The Diary of a Secret Tory MP

The Diary of a
Secret
Tory MP

dodgy
~~Private~~ dispatches from
the heart of Westminster

MUDLARK

For Portillo.
With good behaviour,
you'll be out in five.

Mudlark
HarperCollins*Publishers*
1 London Bridge Street
London SE1 9GF

www.harpercollins.co.uk

HarperCollins*Publishers*
1st Floor, Watermarque Building, Ringsend Road
Dublin 4, Ireland

First published by Mudlark 2022

1 3 5 7 9 10 8 6 4 2

© The Secret Tory MP 2022

The Secret Tory MP asserts the moral right to
be identified as the author of this work

A catalogue record of this book is
available from the British Library

ISBN 978-0-00-853517-9

Printed and bound in the UK using 100%
renewable electricity at CPI Group (UK) Ltd

Author's Note

This is a work of satire. While real individuals are featured, all the events and actions depicted in this book are fiction. I mean, Steve Baker would never take the A355 to Amersham. Everyone knows he takes the A404 via Hazlemere. But just to be clear so no one sues me.

The Secret Tory

'It is a truth universally acknowledged that a single Tory in want of a good fortune must keep a memoir of his life. However little known the views of such a man may be on his first entry to politics, this truth is so well fixed in the minds of the surrounding Tories that without one, he is considered as the rightful property of someone or other of their donors.'

Preface

The idea for an anonymous* journal of my time in Westminster came to me by the heat lamps at Conservative Conference breakfast. As I watched Norman Lamont discreetly putting a sausage in his pocket in the reflection of a laminate egg, I knew I could not end up like him: a once-proud Tory reduced to pilfering offal.

The career of a politician, like that of an elite athlete, is short. One minute you're winning the Tour de France or being returned on eighty-five votes, the next you're failing a drug test. The stark reality for Tories subsisting on eighty-four grand a year is that, unlike with Tiger Woods, Nike will never endorse us, regardless of how many drink-driving arrests or affairs we've had.

---

* All I can tell you is that I drive an Overfinch with an appearance package and 18-inch Apollo wheels.

For a backbencher this is doubly hard. When the day comes that my constituents no longer want me to point at potholes or throw wanker signs across the chamber at Richard Burgon during PMQs, I cannot rely on the UN departmental briefs and Ivy League lecture tours that fall into the laps of ex-ministers caught snogging in cupboards. I must rely on my wits.

Hence I am seizing the initiative. And when, finally, I step back from frontline politics and thrust my hand in my pocket, instead of pulling out a congealed Ramada sausage, I will produce a political journal of such incendiary rambling that it cannot fail to invite a bidding war between Penguin, Simon & Schuster, Bloomsbury, Random House and the woke lunatics at HarperCollins. As you are about to discover, I am Deep Throat, and this is my Watergate.

October 2021

Wednesday, 6 October 2021

Drama on the final day of our conference in Manchester.

What should have been a celebration of the £20 cut to Universal Credit descended into chaos when rumours emerged of a single mother outside the GMEX who had just visited a foodbank, even though she could afford tattoos and was pushing an expensive Maclaren pram.

At least thirty of us piled outside to give her what for.

But it was a trap. She was hypothetical scrounger bait.

A Land Rover driven by deselected centrist patsy Rory Stewart swung out from behind a tram and drenched us by driving through a puddle. His passengers, Nicholas Soames and Ken Clarke, then jeered at us for unilaterally leaving the mutually beneficial union of our peers in the shelter of the hall to look like frothing fools in the outside world.

As Lee Anderson flung a half-eaten kebab at the retreating vehicle and Ben Elliot towelled down his guest Roman Abramovich with a BAE Systems tote bag, I asked myself a philosophical question:

'Like that falling tree in the forest, if an SUV full of centrist melts soaks a pavement full of Brexiteering Tories and nobody is writing a diary about it, does anyone make any money?'

Thursday, 7 October 2021

Late back after Stephen Crabb was sick in Matt Hancock's divorce Subaru at Watford Gap.

Friday, 8 October 2021

Woken by the Burkes' windchimes next door. I swear they're twice as loud when you're on a comedown. It was doubly annoying because they interrupted an excellent dream I was having about Liz Truss. She was walking out of the sea like Ursula Andress in *Dr. No*, but instead of a white bikini in the Caribbean, she was wearing a Union Flag at Dungeness.

Saturday, 9 October 2021

Spent the morning giving out leaflets about economising to the indigents at my local foodbank. Jacob Rees-Mogg came down too and did a flying picket with his children. They piled out of the battered Citroën Xsara Picasso we call the Popemobile and in unbroken cut-glass treble began berating the freeloaders.

After five minutes of shouting, 'Potatoes are cheaper than chips', Jacob became quite agitated and insisted we open every tin of food to ensure no luxury items like foie gras had been secreted inside.

When one of his children, Stephen VI or Boniface (I forget which), asked why, Jacob replied, 'Who knows of what these penne-donating do-gooders are capable?'

Jacob is very wise. But he isn't strong enough to operate the ring-pulls on mass-produced food cans so I had to do it, and by the time we went to Carluccio's for lunch, I was covered in bean juice.

In the evening I drank the WKD Stephen Crabb left here last time his wife kicked him out and watched *Lewis* on ITV4.

Sunday, 10 October 2021

Got a text from Liz Truss today. My heart skipped a beat when I saw her name flash up, but when I opened the message it simply read '?'

I realised I may have texted her when I was drunk last night. I scrolled through my outbox and sure enough, in the middle of fifteen messages to Babestation there was one to the Foreign Secretary.

'Liz, if I'd been a World War II bomber pilot, I'd have painted you on the nose of my Lancaster.'

Monday, 11 October 2021

Boris has gone on holiday again. He'll be fuming when he realises he's missed an opportunity to field questions on the independent report that's damned our Covid response as the *biggest public health failure in history.*

Tuesday, 12 October 2021

Popped into the constituency office. Since I outsourced the operation to Serco and sacked the office manager Portillo (my son), it's been running very smoothly. It didn't at first, but then they re-employed him on half the money and it came good.

The team were in good spirits considering the vandalism over the weekend. Some kids had broken in and smashed up the ceiling tiles in the office so you can now see the sky through the pre-existing roof cavity.

The usual *SHIT TORY BASTARD* and *SCUM* graffiti were there, but there was also a *POVERTY NONCE*, which was quite creative, and *SECRET TORY EATS BIG DINNERS*. I updated the spreadsheet – the thirty-three *SCUM*s this year is a new record – while my volunteers Elsie and Lucy scrubbed it off.

It took them three hours, which is a long time for pensioners to be out in the rain, so I gave them an extra Digestive when they came in for tea. I even offered to let Elsie leave for her MRI fifteen minutes early, but she didn't take me up on it because she wanted to wait until she'd stopped shivering.

Wednesday, 13 October 2021

Boris is still painting in Zac Goldsmith's two-hundred-and-fifty-grand-a-week Marbella tax loophole, so Dom Raab stood in at PMQs with Angela Rayner deputising for Keir. I'm not saying I've got a problem with council estate teen mums from the north who've worked as carers, but every time she spoke Des Swayne and I started humming the *Coronation Street* theme.

Thursday, 14 October 2021

Had another dream about Liz Truss. She was looking all sultry while playing Vladimir Putin at chess. I was so distracted by it that I forgot to take my wallet to work, and by noon was so hungry that I ate the Admiral's Pie that has been in the staff fridge forever.

Friday, 15 October 2021

Massive tension at work. I was shaking the vending machine to release a can of Monster to get me through another tedious meeting about Afghan refugees when Gavin Williamson launched his Luke Skywalker mug against the wall. Thérèse Coffey was trying to calm him down.

'What's wrong?' I asked.

'Someone's eaten Gavin's lunch,' said Thérèse.

'Oh my goodness, that's terrible. What was it?'

'An Admiral's Pie,' whined Gavin.

'It's OK, Gavin, love, people will still think you're an Admiral,' said Thérèse soothingly.

'I'll give you a bit of space, mate,' I said thoughtfully.

In the afternoon I went back to the constituency and did my surgery. One of the regulars, a Falklands veteran called Everton, was waffling on for the umpteenth time about his damp bedsit with the collapsing roof.

'Join the club, mate,' I said, pointing at the hole in our own office ceiling. Then I patiently explained that the lot of a buy-to-let landlord is quite possibly the toughest there is, so he should cut him some slack.

Saturday, 16 October 2021

Really exciting day. One of our favourite Russian donors, Anastasia Volkov, has arranged for me to have a meeting with an arms company called Joburg Munitions Solutions to see if I can do a bit of work for them.

I met the representative, Mick Miller, a real character who told me he'd made his money in DRC blood diamonds, in Giraffe on the South Bank. He said he was looking for someone with a can-do attitude to help him forge new trade corridors in the UK. I was only too happy to help.

This is exactly the kind of buccaneering free trade that Brexit was supposed to foster. And I could do with the extra money because I watched loads of films on Sky Box Office last month and my direct debit is going to be massive.

Sunday, 17 October 2021

Owen Paterson rang and asked if I had a minute to chat because he thinks he's going to be found guilty of lobbying, but I was late for an appointment at Halfords to get a

Passchendaele vinyl wrap on the Overfinch, so I told him I didn't.

Monday, 18 October 2021

Portillo wasn't in the office today, which was annoying because I've got over 20,000 unread messages and I've been meaning to ask him to show me how to send the ones from my constituents straight to junk.

They're never important, just bleating about delayed Universal Credit payments, houses unfit for human habitation and Covid. It's always the Leftwaffe. Tories only ever message about ways to bend planning regulations.

Nonetheless, I diligently managed to reply to a couple of the Covid messages before I got bored, saying that it's no worse than the flu and that they should man up and trust our proven track record of handling this pandemic.

Tuesday, 19 October 2021

Highest daily cases since March.

Wednesday, 20 October 2021

Went for lunch with the Environment Minister George Eustice at the Aberdeen Angus Steakhouse. He showed me some fantastic stats which said that water companies had discharged raw sewage into our rivers over 400,000 times last year.

It's so life-affirming to think that with every single release of treacly brown effluent, these private firms are putting their shareholders' interest above the public.

'It's a tribute to Tory principles,' said George.

'Tributary,' I quipped.

'That's good. You're wasted in politics.'

'I agree.'

We drank several toasts to monopolised water, then, a bit giddy, went in to vote to keep it legal for privatised utilities to discharge as much shit into our waterways as they like.

Thursday, 21 October 2021

Saw Liz Truss outside Black Rod's office. She asked me to stop texting her when I was drunk. I was going to ask if she was still driving her pink Renault Twingo, but tripped and fell into Chris Bryant instead.

Friday, 22 October 2021

Portillo had cleared today's diary for me to have a crucial meeting with the husband of one of my constituents who has been taken hostage in Iran. However, I was tired and needed some me time, so I cancelled and drove a soothing circuit of the M25 instead.

Saturday, 23 October 2021

Realised I'd left my vape on the fruit machines at Clacket Lane Roadchef yesterday, so climbed back into the Overfinch after *Saturday Kitchen* and returned to ask if anyone had picked it up.

There was nobody near the slots, so I went into WHSmith.

'Dave, have we got any more copies of *BBC History Magazine*?' said a striking estuary accent from the store-room.

'No, that Neil Oliver keeps coming in and buying them all. Jodie, did you pick up a vape off the fruities yesterday?'

'Did it have Union Jacks on?'

'Yeah,' I shouted, voluntarily mimicking her dropped 's' because I know how to interact with social classes C2 to E, 'that's it.'

'Yeah, hang on a minute, then.'

I browsed the inflatable neck rests and hand fans, eagerly waiting for the owner of the voice to emerge. And it was worth the wait. Imagine Linda Lusardi in her pomp but with tattooed knuckles. I haven't felt time stand still like that since Steve Barclay bet me I couldn't eat five Sara Lees in one sitting. She put down a crate of Yazoo and handed me the vape.

'Aren't you that guy off the TV?'

'*Politics Live? Good Morning Britain? Have I Got News for You?*'

'The *Panorama* investigation into illegal animal testing.'

'Yes. I mean yeah. But that was a long time ago …'

'Thought so. It's the nose.'

In that instant, I knew my feelings for Liz Truss were mere schoolboy infatuation: this was love.

I tried to say something witty, but incredibly, nothing came out. Sensing the commuters behind me becoming impatient I lurched for a grab bag of Sizzling King Prawn McCoy's.

'Just these, please,' I whispered, even though I prefer Thai Sweet Chicken.

She rang them through the till in silence. I left.

Had I just let my first shot at love since walking Katie Hopkins back to her Travelodge after a Dover Is Full rally slip through my fingers?

I was so preoccupied I even allowed myself to get cut up by a Nova at the Wisley interchange. And not even tailgating it to South Mimms could make me feel any better.

Sunday, 24 October 2021

Didn't sleep well, then woke up to find social media full of people complaining about water companies discharging sewage into rivers. Who knew that siding with faeces over people would run you into committed opposition?

From where I'm sitting, as a non-executive director of Thames Water, the clean-water lobby is a malign influence on our national discourse.

Chief Whip Mark Spencer shared a 'This should shut them up' template email for the Andrew Bridgens of this world to send out. It said that this was how things had to be, for ever, because it would cost six hundred billion pounds to upgrade our infrastructure.

Monday, 25 October 2021

Got an inbox full of messages pointing out that I should have deleted 'This should shut them up' from the subject line of my email and that it will cost sixty, not six hundred billion, to fix our sewers. Coincidently, this is the same sum water companies have paid to shareholders since privatisation. Determined to get to grips with the problem once and for all, I rang Portillo and asked him when he was going to stop my constituents emailing me.

Tuesday, 26 October 2021

We've performed an unprecedented U-turn on the environment bill. Feeling helpless, but like I wanted to fight back, I evacuated as much patriotism as possible into the Aitken Suite, my downstairs loo, in the hope some of it might be in an SSSI by midnight. I texted Brandon Lewis during *Newsnight* and he replied, 'Great minds.' He'd just done exactly the same thing.

Wednesday, 27 October 2021

Went for a traditional budget-day breakfast with John Whittingdale. He's great fun. I love hearing about the latest taxpayer-funded dominatrix he's got on the go.

He was wearing a bearskin ushanka and insisted on buying vodka because the Russians had just donated another twenty-five grand to his constituency. He told me that he was still 'Barry Buzzing' after smuggling a packet of Randoms into HMP Leyhill for disgraced MP and sexual predator Charlie Elphicke last month.

I tried to compete with his thrilling anecdote by telling him I'd just parked in a disabled bay.

But this was a mistake, because he started saying, 'Are you a naughty Tory? I'm a naughty Tory,' which became very annoying by the time I realised that he wasn't going to say anything else.

Not as annoying as the ticket that was waiting for me when I came back outside, though. I went ballistic and told the parking warden that I hoped she had a young family because I was going to take great pleasure in putting all of them out on the street.

She looked terrified, especially when a voice behind me said, 'He's a naughty Tory.'

During the budget itself Rishi did all that empathy stuff, saying that he only got into politics to make the world a better place and that 'the first thousand days of a child's life are the most important'.

When he said that, IDS leant across and whispered, 'I always remember that first thousand days figure because it's the same as the number of Sure Start centres we've closed since taking office.'

A good budget, all in. My ideological colleagues were upset by the taxation and spending, but for those of us who care about nothing other than power for its own sake, it did the trick.

Afterwards, Rishi was swanning around in front of the lobby journalists on College Green with the Labrador his image consultant told him to get. It certainly worked. Even ferocious media pit bull Peston was grilling him on Nova's dog food rather than the bankers' levy.

Thursday, 28 October 2021

Andrew Bridgen came into Westminster wearing a large novelty badge and waving a birthday card he'd got from Boris. Most of us humoured him, but when Theresa Villiers told him that Allegra sends them out on Boris's behalf on all our birthdays he started crying and we felt bad.

To make him feel better Esther McVey reminded him about the *Go Jetters* cake Nevena had sent in for him to give out to his friends. I couldn't have any on account of doing Rishi a favour by taking Nova to be euthanised because he didn't need it any more.

Friday, 29 October 2021

Portillo managed to get the PM to come to a meeting with the annoying husband of that woman who has been taken hostage in Iran. When I looked at the man's tired, wretched face I thought, *Being PM has really taken it out of you.* Then I turned to my constituent, and it dawned on me that, neither of us could ever truly know happiness until we were with the women we loved. Whether that was a wife of sixteen years wrongfully imprisoned by the Islamist regime in Tehran or a girl who works on the tills at Clacket Lane Roadchef, we were in the same boat.

So I made my apologies and left the meeting to go and declare my undying love for Jodie.

Although, due to a contraflow at Hanger Lane, she'd knocked off by the time I got there, so I left my number on some HoC headed paper and had a go in a massage chair instead.

Saturday, 30 October 2021

The French have taken one of our fishing trawlers hostage. Liz Truss has summoned the French Ambassador to stop the Frogs pursuing their insane plan of making us adhere to international agreements. The Trawler Wars have begun!

Mark Francois put out a call on 1922 Committee WhatsApp for all able-bodied members to come and train with his paintball team Apocalypse Delta Force.

I picked up James Cleverly and Bill Cash at noon and we drove to Mark's house in Rayleigh to get the bibs. After ringing his doorbell for several minutes, we pressed our faces to the stained-glass Help4Heroes UPVC and saw a semi-naked form motionless on the floor.

'Mark!' screamed James.

A quick-thinking Cash shoulder-barged the door and we waded through a sea of empty Bombay Bad Boy Pot Noodles to Mark's prostrate form. He was unresponsive. I grabbed a can of Relentless from his fridge and, with James cradling his head, used it to revive him.

Mark sat up with a start, his glasses sitting diagonally across his face.

'Don't let Barnier take the haddock!' he said groggily. We cheered.

After coming round, Gino explained that he had been practising dressing up as a frogman in case he needed to be deployed to rescue the trawler in a hurry. However, he'd struggled to get his leg into the wetsuit, began hopping around the kitchen and ended up knocking himself cold on the table.

We didn't leave until he could reel off the name of every crew member on the Dams Raid, at which point we took off his scuba mask, tucked him into his Fighter Command duvet and stepped out into the still October air, relieved that our comrade had survived what was technically the first engagement of the Trawler War.

Sunday, 31 October 2021

Carved a Trident submarine into my pumpkin. It's three times bigger than the Burkes' next door, which they've painted in rainbow colours. When I pointed this out through the leylandii I planted so I don't have to watch them doing al fresco Pilates, they ignored me.

The trick or treaters started at noon. Like last year, they were mainly focused on throwing fireworks at my house. But what the little tykes, their parents and I think a grand-parent didn't realise is that a sustained pyrotechnic assault on the house of an MP at war with France is water off a duck's back. Indeed, should I get trapped behind enemy lines in an executive detached new-build on the edge of Le Havre, it will have been the perfect training.

The barrage subsided at nine when Londis ran out of fireworks, at which point I felt comfortable switching my doorbell from Air Raid to All Clear.

November 2021

Monday, 1 November 2021

Some unionist gunmen blew up a bus in County Down this morning, which I think is a tribute to David Frost's negotiating skills.

Luckily it didn't overshadow COP26, our last chance to save life on earth until the next one. I'm excited and worried in equal measure. On the one hand man-made climate change doesn't exist. On the other, it's an opportunity for Boris to strut around on the world stage. Indeed, Joe Biden and Angela Merkel were so blown away by his amazing speech about global warming being like James Bond five–nil down at a minute to midnight, they started laughing.

As for the detail, I had no idea what anyone was talking about. My position is this: if voters want me to look like I care about man-made climate change, I'm going to look like

I care about man-made climate change. And even if it is real, I'm not worried. The sheer volume of private jets on display surely means we're confident we can fix it.

Tuesday, 2 November 2021

Trawler victory! The French couldn't cope with the threat of deployment of ERG special forces. That and the hundred extra fishing licences we issued.

Matt Hancock and the Crabbmeister rang and said I should come with them on a booze cruise to Calais because the local girls would be throwing themselves at us for liberating them. I wasn't interested … because Jodie texted!

'Got ur number from Dean at Clacket. Wht u want?'

'I came in last week to get my vape and I just wanted to say thanks because it was still full, so you clearly hadn't used it. I'm tied up making decisions crucial to the future of the country this week, but when I'm not, would you like to do something?'

'Gr8 that ur busy. Y.'

'Yes, I am very busy. Would you like to come to an event with me next Saturday?'

'Y if I can get mum to have the kids.'

I was so happy I took a Strawberry Müller Corner from the fridge to celebrate.

Wednesday, 3 November 2021

Politics is such an up and down business. One minute you're organising a street party in honour of a million liberated turbot, the next you're going in to bat for a colleague a cross-party group of MPs has found guilty of breaking lobbying rules, taking nearly three times his MPs' salary in paid advocacy, and smearing the commissioner investigating him. The Owen Paterson lobbying non-story has broken.

I vaguely remembered him saying something to me about it on the phone a couple of weeks ago, but like his interests, it didn't register.

Even so, if there's one thing I loathe it's injustice, and I decided I would not rest until I had exonerated the honourable member for North Shropshire and arranged a clandestine meeting with the Leader of the House Jacob Rees-Mogg and Chief Whip Mark Spencer in the bathing ponds on Hampstead Heath. Together, we hatched a plan tighter than Eric Pickles' G-string. It is this:

We will say that the parliamentary standards commission urgently needs overhauling. This will nullify Owen's conviction, and nobody will notice or care because they didn't seem to mind when our neglect killed tens of thousands of their relatives. It will have the bonus of getting several other of our colleagues off the hook, including the most investigated man in Parliament, Boris Johnson. Boris was thrilled with the idea and pushed a three-line whip on a hastily drafted amendment to which Andrea Leadsom happily put her name, even though she hadn't read it.

Despite the whinnying of the woke contingent opposite it passed easily, and Owen was reprieved until such a time as we can establish a suitably toothless organisation to absolve him. Another great day for UK democracy.

Thursday, 4 November 2021

Everything has gone mental. Kwasi Kwarteng went on the breakfast rounds to defend our plan, doubling down and suggesting that it was actually the head of the standards commission Kathryn Stone who should be considering her position. So far so good. But by mid-morning, noticing that more people than usual were incandescent with fury, the PM performed another unprecedented U-turn.

As the news came through, many of my ideologically afflicted colleagues were upset that they had been hung out to dry by the whipped vote.

'How could we have been betrayed by a man who arranged for his friend to get beaten up by Darius Guppy?' asked Dehenna Davison.

'Why didn't Marina Wheeler, the wife he left for another woman while she was undergoing cancer treatment, warn us?' asked Scott Benton.

'The amendment was in my name. That means Leadsom

could become a byword for arrant stupidity,' complained Andrea Leadsom.

I stormed into the sports massage Boris was having with Harry Cole and demanded to know what had happened. He explained that the plan wasn't as watertight as we'd thought because it required Labour to support the new standards commission. I couldn't for the life of me understand how Jacob, author of *The Victorians* ('A staggeringly silly book'), could have missed such a detail.

I looked at Harry, who looked at Boris and said, 'You're very tense in your scapula, Sarge. I think we should do some more release work.'

At this point Kwasi walked in, genuflected and began to clean Boris's shoes.

'Whatever you need me to go out and say or do on TV Boris, I'll do it.' He looked at the floor. 'I'd say anything for you.'

It has all been very discombobulating. None of us are very used to encountering the consequences of our actions.

Friday, 5 November 2021

This evening I headed out to Biggleswade for Nadine's infamous annual fireworks. After the week we've just had, singing 'Rule, Britannia!' while the 21st Bedfordshire Guides burned an effigy of James O'Brien on a bonfire of books about critical race theory was just the tonic.

Saturday, 6 November 2021

The morale boost was brief. Graham Brady has sent round an email promising vengeance on whoever took his Strawberry Müller Corner.

Sunday, 7 November 2021

Popped over to Gospel Oak to check up on my taxpayer-funded nest egg. It's a five-bedroomed flat overlooking Hampstead Heath which I keep comfortingly empty during this time of unprecedented housing pressure.

While I was there I heard John Major on the radio accusing Boris of riding roughshod over standards in public life. I always knew he was a Trotskyist. What did Edwina Currie ever see in the bespectacled milquetoast? I was so angry I resolved to lobby extra hard for Joburg Munition Solutions at the MOD tomorrow.

Monday, 8 November 2021

Pleasant commute to the procurement meeting in Whitehall listening to Def Leppard while familiarising myself with Heckler & Koch MP5s and Spike LR2 anti-tank guided missiles.

Upon arrival I was directed down an alley and instructed to climb in through a kitchen window, a preventative measure against any confusion that might arise from people who don't know how arms dealing works.

Once inside I was made to feel very at home. I explained to General Sir Bernard Fairfax that with my extensive experience on 1996 PC game *Command & Conquer: Red Alert*, we had a lot in common as battlefield commanders.

He let me wear his hat and I even got him to show me the Trident codes. They're the names of Boris's children, which worries the top brass because they don't know if he'll be able to remember them all if we need to launch in a hurry.

It was all very productive, and I even did them a two for one on some fragmentation mines. We had a good laugh when I started climbing back out of the window too. I'd forgotten to take off Sir Bernard's hat! Imagine if I'd turned up to an emergency debate on parliamentary sleaze wearing a general's hat I'd borrowed during an illegal arms meeting.

Tuesday, 9 November 2021

Went to Geoffrey Cox's office to give him a receipt for a pint of milk.

'You'll have earned a hundred quid in the time it takes to submit that for expenses, Geoff,' I said as I passed it to the aide who holds the tablet he dials in on.

'If you look after the pennies, the pounds will look after themselves,' replied the sonorous QC.

'Nice background,' I said, pointing at the sun-kissed sea behind him.

'It's not a background. I'm on Rod Stewart's yacht.'

'Oh. Lovely. Whereabouts?'

'The British Virgin Islands. I'm defending their government on corruption charges.'

Wednesday, 10 November 2021

Apropos of nothing, Boris felt compelled to go back to COP26 to give the delegates another important climate-related message: 'The UK is not a remotely corrupt country.'

Afterwards, Geoffrey Clifton-Brown joked in ERG WhatsApp that if you say 'The UK is not a remotely corrupt country' in a mirror three times it turns into a Zoom with Coxy.

Later, Andrew Bridgen wrote, 'Not being funny, Geoff, but I've been trying this for three hours and it isn't true.'

There is a tangible mood of distrust among my colleagues at the moment. Penny Mordaunt's Quorn lasagne has been stolen from the fridge. We're all eyeing each other suspiciously, wondering whether the Tory we are talking to is capable of stealing food out of a hungry mouth.

Matt Hancock has been appointed to head up an investigation to get to the bottom of it. When Labour found out they were outraged.

'You've set up an investigation to find an internal food thief before you've even done one to look at your handling of Covid,' said Rosena Allin-Khan.

'You can't work on an empty stomach, Rachel,' replied Boris.

There are a lot of names flying about. Nadine Dorries thinks it's Theresa May trying to undermine Boris's mandate; Thérèse Coffey thinks it's Tom Tugendhat because she once offered him her breakfast Pringles and he took twenty; and pretty much everyone else thinks Michael Gove has something to do with it.

Whatever happens, Boris's authority within the parliamentary party is shot until he fixes it. I'm just glad it wasn't me this time.

Thursday, 11 November 2021

Remembrance Day. Left a pork pie on my patio for the Unknown Soldier, then went into town to object to people not observing the minute's silence. I'm taking Jodie out tomorrow, so I went to Orvis and bought a pair of plum cords and a new quilted gilet too.

When I got into work, I overheard Matt Hancock shaking down Danny Kruger about the stolen lunches. Turns out it wasn't a Quorn lasagne that went missing after all. It was a cottage pie. Now I come to think about it, I did eat one of those.

Friday, 12 November 2021

Date with Jodie. I was at Clacket Lane for two but due to unforeseen European labour shortages she had to work late. When she eventually finished, I produced a box of All Gold.

'I was going to give these to Liz Truss.'

'Who the fuck is Liz Truss?'

'A social-media influencer and Foreign Secretary. There's only five missing.'

'Never heard of her. I prefer Heroes.'

I was mesmerised. 'We're a bit late so don't worry about getting changed out of your uniform.'

'Fine. Where are we going?'

'Chequers.'

We only just made it in time for the reception due to the ongoing barrier works at Hanger Lane, the nuances of which I explained to President Biden as he sipped champagne and I finished the Lucozade Sport from my lunchtime meal deal.

Jodie was quite brilliant. She and Carrie got on like a house on fire, bonding over interior design and the relative trials of budgeting for eight-hundred-quid-a-roll Lulu Lytle wallpaper and BrightHouse sofa repayments at 70 per cent APR.

When we tried to leave, the car wouldn't start, I suspect because I ran the battery down listening to Rod Stewart covering Oasis songs while waiting for Jodie. I wandered back in to ask for help, inadvertently interrupting Joe Biden telling Boris he'd 'have to initiate Article 16 over the dead bodies of Marine Force Recon'.

Boris shouted at me to get out, then told Allegra to find him a 'fucking room, nowhere near' me.

When I explained to Jodie that we were spending the night of our first date in the Belgrano Suite at the Prime Minister's country residence, she dealt with any potential awkwardness by draining her can of Tetley's, heading it into the bin and saying, 'Sound, I'm shagged. Nice to meet you, Kamala. You never told me what you did?'

I won't lie, when we got to our room I was wondering if something was going to happen, but as I approached the bed Jodie set my mind at ease by saying, 'No chance, sofa.'

Saturday, 13 November 2021

In the morning we went down for breakfast. Eggs sunny-side up and over easy for the Americans, Benedict for the Brits and Cookie Crisp for the PM. He was late down, but raised voices drifted ahead.

'Don't ever touch my fucking phone again.'

'I can't believe you're still shagging her.'

'Why wouldn't I? You're too busy with that fucking kid.'

'Oh my god. Our kid.'

'Whatever.'

'You just don't care for anything because you're spoilt. You're only happy if you're in a scrape you have to find your way out of. It's pathetic.'

'Is it?'

'Yes.'

'Why don't you fuck off back to Guido or Harry then. I can find a million more just like you.'

'Where, IT support? PC World?'

'Whatever.'

'Currys?'

'Oh fuck off. If you want to keep a roof over, what's he called? Wilfred? Wilfred's head, mop up that mascara, get your game face on, and come and feed Joe his puréed breakfast.'

Then they entered. Initially it was awkward, but sensing something needed doing, our consummate leader drained the milk from his cereal bowl, sprang from his chair, said, 'Watch this,' and proceeded to attempt some sit-ups.

Over the laughter and chants from his aides of 'Boris, Boris', a man in overalls tapped me on the shoulder.

'Do you drive the Overfinch?'

I leant back casually. 'Eighteen-inch Apollo alloys?'

'Yes.'

'Guilty.'

'Right. Well, it's ready.'

'OK, cheers mate. Jodie, that's us.'

Kamala saw what was happening and approached Boris, who was now supinated in the manner of an upended beetle.

'Hey, Boris, can't Jodie stay? I like her, I feel like we've got so much to talk about.'

'I'm not sure,' wheezed the G7 leader as he propped himself up on his elbows.

'Oh, c'mon, Bozzy. It might help us iron out a few more details on this trade deal you guys definitely aren't desperate for.'

And so, while Boris and Joe held crucial talks about the future of our respective nations and Kamala, Carrie and Jodie walked Dilyn around the grounds of Chequers, I watched *The Rock* in the cinema room with the American Secret Service. The ultimate end to a first date.

'Would you like to do this again?' I asked as I dropped Jodie for her afternoon shift.

'Maybe. Bye.'

And she was gone.

Sunday, 14 November 2021

Spent the day drinking Tetley's to remind myself of Jodie.

Monday, 15 November 2021

There was an article in the paper saying that every time a Tory donor hits the £3 million mark they are made a peer of the realm and get to legislate in the House of Lords. I wrote a letter to the *Express* offering a solution – Peerometers. Those big-money thermometer things you have on *Blue Peter*, but placed outside the houses of Tory stooges and Russian oligarchs, so that the public can keep tabs on how close they are getting towards legislating over us.

Tuesday, 16 November 2021

Nadine Dorries made me come for lunch with her. It was fun in the bits when she wasn't on her phone talking dirty to some bloke called Alexander, or telling the manager that unless he wanted the full weight of the DCMS brought to bear on his twelve-seat bistro he needed to sack our waiter.

Wednesday, 17 November 2021

Needed a phone upgrade so I switched my constituency surgery to the Carphone Warehouse at the last minute, which had the extra advantage of almost nobody turning up for it.

Only Everton found me, which in itself was quite helpful because when I was about to get a Galaxy S7 he intervened and recommended the excellent Z Flip3. I thanked him for the advice and asked if there was anything I could do to help him. He told me that his landlord had been over and propped up the sagging roof of his bedsit with a broom handle balanced on a chair and charged him for it. It's a rotten situation. So I took him to Greggs to try and once more explain the struggles that landlords face. Then I let him buy me a steak bake because it was good for his confidence.

Thursday, 18 November 2021

Back-to-back meetings all day. Spent most of them pretending to listen while secretly arguing in the comments on YouTube child-car-seat-installation videos on my new phone. Then I texted Jodie and asked if she'd like to come driven grouse shooting next weekend. Reader, she said yes.

Friday, 19 November 2021

I saw Olly Dowden while I was trying to dislodge a packet of Fruit Polos from the knackered old vending machine in the lobby. He said that party co-chair Ben Elliot was organising a luxury fundraising night for Russian Tory donors through his company Quintessentially, and was wondering if I'd like to come along.

I tried not to look too flattered. Ben's concierge service for oligarchs – doing everything from booking restaurant tables to securing backstage access to pop stars, and from arranging golden passports to introing them to the UK's most creative accounting schemes – is highly regarded. The people who use it are some of the most supremely dubious individuals in the world.

'Can I think about it?' I said, playing it cool.

'Yes, but I need to know by mid-afternoon or I'll ask Ben Bradley.'

'I've thought about it, and I'll definitely be there.'

'Super. I'll add you to the Hammer and Sicklephants WhatsApp.'

He swung his bum into the vending machine, dislodged my Polos and winked at me.

'Stick with Olly D, Secret. There's plenty more where that came from. See you tomorrow.'

Saturday, 20 November 2021

The dinner was at Alisher Usmanov's £25 million Sutton Place Tudor mansion.

But when I arrived, instead of being shown into the spectacular main room to mingle with the likes of Roman

Abramovich, Anastasia Volkov, Yevgeny Prigozhin, Andrey Kostin, Nikolai Tokarev and Dmitri Lebedev (sadly no Arron Banks), I was unceremoniously shoved below stairs with Simon Clarke, Alun Cairns, Brandon Lewis, Chris Heaton-Harris and Conor Burns.

Carrie was handing out novelty collars and bow ties.

'Strip.'

'What?'

'Strip. Take your shirts off and put these on.'

'Roman didn't buy Chelsea because he cares about football. Prigozhin doesn't run a private army of far-right mercenaries for fun. These Russians pay very good money to get access to legislators like you. They want influence. And topless waiters,' said Ben.

'But that's degrading,' said Conor Burns.

Ben and Carrie both laughed.

'Brandon's twenty grand, Chris's twenty, your ten, Alun's five …' – we sniggered at the small sum – 'you don't think they give that to you for nothing?' asked Ben.

'They give it to us because they admire us,' said Brandon primly.

'You can't possibly believe that,' said Carrie. Ben opened a door to a velvet-lined bedroom where Daniel Kerchingski was washing Dmitri Lebedev's feet.

'Tell them, Dan.'

'We've all got to do our bit.'

Ben closed the door again.

'I'm really not sure,' said Chris.

'I'm the co-chair of the Tory Party. Do you know what that means?'

'That you have to listen to Oliver Dowden humming showtunes all day?' said Brandon.

'No. Well, yes. But also, it means I've got to keep the coffers full. Which means keeping Russians happy. So, get your shirts off, get these bow ties on, and start serving your Masters their Margaritas.'

It wasn't so bad. I mean, it was one of the most humiliating experiences of my life, my belly sagging over my belt as Evgeny Lebedev prodded my moobs with Twiglets, but as Alun Cairns pointed out on one of our kitchen resupply trips, it was no worse than the aftermath of Mike Fabricant's fiftieth in that youth hostel.

I felt particularly sorry for six-foot-eight Simon Clarke, who can't conceivably have thought the ten-grand donation to his constituency office was worth Usmanov insisting he crawl around on all fours and 'bark like a little Teesside doggy' every time someone said freeport.

Towards the end of the night I did feel as if I was starting to recover some of my dignity, when lovely Anastasia Volkov introduced me to Yevgeny Prigozhin.

I was serving a St Basil's configuration platter of BBQ Pringles when she invited me to sit down. With nowhere else to put it, I placed the giant salver on my crotch.

She began asking me questions about myself, which was pleasant after an evening of degradation, and Yevgeny said that he was wondering if I might like to do some work with him and our mutual friend Mick Miller from Joburg Munitions Enterprises.

'Well, of course. But I thought it was "Joburg Munitions Solutions"?'

'Mick likes to rebrand every few weeks or so,' said Anastasia.

They started going into the details, at which point my mind began to do that thing it often does when people go into details: not listening. In this instance it was because I couldn't help noticing a tantalising glimpse of bra between the buttonholes of Anastasia's taffeta blouse, and despite invoking the memory of David Mellor in nothing but a Chelsea shirt, the Pringles began to slide towards one end of the salver. There was a baffled pause. Then Yevgeny and Anastasia looked at each other and laughed.

'Mr Tory, is that an illegally acquired gun in your pocket, or are you just pleased to see me?' said Anastasia.

'A bit of both,' I gulped.

'Well, I'm afraid to say I'm married to a man who is very good friends with Mr Putin, and were you to impugn my honour, he would not hesitate to take you to the Salisbury Cathedral visitor centre. If you know what I mean?'

'Not really,' I whispered.

They stood up.

'I'll be in touch,' snarled Yevgeny, before bending down, taking a hyperbolic paraboloid of reconstituted potato from the tray and crunching it open-mouthed in my face.

Sunday, 21 November 2021

Olly rang to ask how things went. I omitted the bit about the psychological scarring and said it was fine.

Saw on the news that Putin has begun massing troops on the Ukrainian border. I don't think anything will happen. The prospect of Putin daring to cross Boris, the man who put the son of a KGB colonel in the House of Lords against the advice of his own security services, is so improbable as not to be worth thinking about.

Monday, 22 November 2021

Boris gave a scintillating speech to the CBI today. Comparing himself to Moses, he said that Mother Nature doesn't like us working from home, and after losing his place went on a rambling detour about Peppa Pig World. After two weeks of being pulverised by constituents over shitty rivers and endemic corruption, it was exactly the sort of Churchillian oratory the captains of industry needed.

Tuesday, 23 November 2021

Got my decorations up today and now I really am in the Christmas spirit. There's nothing like an LED nativity on the side of your mock Tudor car port to remind you that mince pies, a TV schedule identical to last year, and a tidal wave of new-variant Covid about which we are going to do nothing are only just around the corner.

Wednesday, 24 November 2021

Twenty-seven people have died in the Channel. I tried to cry but I couldn't because they were economic migrants. It made me reflect on the nativity story. If it teaches us anything it is that Mary and Joseph should have gone through proper immigration channels rather than making a perilous journey to an inn which was oversubscribed because the locals were too busy looking after their own.

I think the Bible talks the whole thing up a bit, to be honest. Like when it says that they then 'fled' to Egypt to escape Herod's purge of the infants – how do we know they weren't actually just after forty quid a week and a mobile?

Thursday, 25 November 2021

Turns out the economic migrants who perished in the Channel were Kurds who'd left behind the glamorous world of war with Turkey and Syria to come here in the hope of fleecing a system into which I don't pay any tax.

'This is a result of an immigration policy that incentivises people with the offer of five quid a day to live in Salford Precinct,' I said to Jodie on the phone while trying to arrange our grouse shooting weekend.

'You do realise that by ignoring the powerful reasons these people have to make them risk everything, and by persistently using degrading language to describe them, you're dehumanising yourself as well as them?'

It was an interesting point, so I ignored it.

Friday, 26 November 2021

Grouse shooting.

Forgot to cancel my surgery, so I killed two birds with one stone to kill several hundred with a shotgun, and asked Everton to take it on my behalf. He's attended more of them than I have recently, so nobody has a better idea of what's required, including me, if I'm honest.

Then I picked Jodie up and we drove to Stansted. She asked if flying to Yorkshire during a climate crisis was wise.

I explained that driven grouse shooting is so good for the environment it actually offsets the flight. Yes, the DGS community might be burning moorland, and yes, damaged peatland might be responsible for 5 per cent of the world's greenhouse-gas emissions, but when you think of the conservation gains made by employing gamekeepers to exterminate all the local wildlife, the rewards are obvious.

At Leeds Bradford we were greeted by a Hummer and driven to the Nidderdale raptor black hole and Viscount Rapacity's Thruscross Estate. We were shown into a grand eighteenth-century hall where, beneath the terrifying twenty-foot pictures of the Viscount's slaver ancestors, we attended a reception with the usual mix of oligarchs, Saudi princes and Ian Botham. Jodie listened with interest as Beefy bragged that the last time he'd been on a moor he'd got so drunk he bagged thirty grouse and a peregrine without a memory of firing a single shot.

In the evening the Viscount hosted a dinner of gamebirds and game birds, the latter blonde and from Eastern Europe. Jodie sat between Sir Edward Leigh and the arms dealer Wafic Said and regaled them with an anecdote of the time she was involved in a police pursuit on the A406, throwing bags of Es out of the sunroof of her Fiat Panda.

I sat between two women called Svetlana and Dagmar. They took a keen interest in me and cried tears of laughter into their woodcock as I told them how the Trident codes were named after the PM's children.

Saturday, 27 November 2021

Woke with a splitting headache. Nothing happened with Jodie last night on account of her telling me, 'If I'd wanted to get mugged off by a pair of East European slags, I'd have gone out in Dagenham.'

I explained that they weren't Eastern European; they were Russian; and it was precisely because she wasn't revealing all her cleavage that I respected her to the point of not talking to her all evening. At which juncture, in her wall of silence, the gamekeepers arrived to pick us up in their Gators.

After a thrilling drive up onto the moor and several nips of the Viscount's forty-year-old Dalmore, or in my case Aftershock (red), we were installed in the butts.

Driven grouse shooting is a highly skilled endeavour, popularised by the royal family in the nineteenth century, in which you use a conveyer belt of preloaded shotguns to shoot a flock of medicated birds out of the sky. In terms of sporting prowess, it's darts without the skill or fitness, and in many ways is a microcosm of the British class system, requiring large numbers of poor people, vast tracts of land and a substantial amount of collateral death to facilitate the enjoyment of a handful of insecure ultra-wealthy men.

On the first drive I winged three birds. Jodie hit fifteen. The gamekeepers were very impressed. But on the second an endangered hen harrier began quartering the moor, and so discouraged the grouse from flying up into our sights.

Everyone was furious. Beefy said that if this had happened on his moor, he'd have given the keeper a thick ear. Viscount Rapacity, not wanting to be outdone, sacked the head keeper on the spot, then produced a sniper rifle and despatched the functionally extinct bird himself.

All told, it was a wonderful day in the field and, apart from repeatedly having to remind Jodie not to talk to the beaters (a mixture of the rural poor and forelock-tugging police and Conservative councillors who think wearing tweed is a personality trait), a complete success.

When the bags were read out at dinner Jodie was streets ahead of everyone else. We all coped with being beaten by a woman (it's the twenty-first century after all), apart from Chris Chope, who shouted, 'Object!', pushed over a suit of armour and locked himself in his room.

Things were going well with Jodie again, so I even decided I was going to talk to her during dinner. She was particularly interested in hearing me discuss all the Christmas parties I went to at Downing Street last year.

After the cheese, Viscount Rapacity suggested the women leave so that the strippers could come in. Jodie gave me a long, searching look, almost as if what I was about to say would determine the future of our relationship. 'There's a TV in the room, love; you could go and watch *8 out of 10 Cats Does Countdown* if you like?'

Sunday, 28 November 2021

Woke up with a throbbing head and Jodie nowhere to be seen.

I stumbled to the window and looked out. Across the courtyard, she was helping the family of the sacked game-keeper move their possessions from the cottage that came with the job into a van. I lifted the sash.

'Jodie, he almost ruined a thirty-two-grand shoot for sixteen Tories. He deserves everything that's coming to him.'

She didn't hear me. She didn't seem to hear me at break-fast, either. Or in the car to the airport. Or during the flight home. Or when she got out at Clacket Lane and I asked when she'd next like to see me. It was all very odd.

Monday, 29 November 2021

Very blue about how things went with Jodie. I couldn't focus on anything and accidently sent an email intended for Mike Fabricant to an Iranian minister saying that I thought it was likely the woman in prison in Tehran was a spy because I've met her husband and he's a teacher who wears cords.

Sir Edward Leigh saw I was looking glum and walked me up to the Bomber Command Memorial at Marble Arch to watch Johnny Mercer do his lunchtime exercises. He pointed out that all that coke Viscount Rapacity insisted we sniff off his upturned J. M. W. Turners might have had something to do with it.

'But what about Jodie? I just don't understand. Was she upset that I barely talked to her all weekend? Does she think eviscerating birds with gouty men is a rubbish date? Maybe she objected to me letting Graham Brady get a lap dance in our en suite at three in the morning? I just don't understand.'

Sir Edward fixed me with his compassionate gaze.

'Listen, Secret Tory. Women come and go. But friendships with Tories forged in sordid situations that can never become public: they last a lifetime.'

Then we hugged. I think he might be the most emotionally intelligent man I know.

Tuesday, 30 November 2021

When I got to the constituency office Everton was there scrubbing off the weekend's graffiti.

Now that is a good idea, I thought to myself. *Hats off to Portillo for keeping him out of the sort of trouble veterans on state benefits are so often seduced by.*

But all was not as it seemed. Apparently, Everton had solved so much backlogged casework at my surgery that Portillo had invited him back to do some more, but when he saw Lucy and Elsie doing the weekly graffiti scrub in the freezing weather he insisted they go inside while he cleaned it all himself.

I ordered him to desist at once. Elsie and Lucy might look the part, with their bottles of Cillit Bang hanging from their snazzy Zimmer frames, but they work slowly, and if they become accustomed to taking time off they'll get out of practice. He apologised and asked if I'd managed to contact his landlord.

'I'm afraid not, Everton. I've been up against it.'

December 2021

Wednesday, 1 December 2021

The new Omicron variant is making everyone very excitable. Steve Baker thinks we're charting a course 'away from salvation and straight to hell' if we ask people to wear facemasks in Sainsbury's. I thought this was a bit odd considering the top of his website says 'I believe everyone has a moral duty to sustain life'. But regardless, Steve is led by God and wherever the C&A Evangelist goes, the rest of us must follow.

Thursday, 2 December 2021

The *Mirror* has released the story about Boris having Christmas parties and regular end-of-week drinks parties during both lockdowns. They seemed to think it was some sort of scoop, but I don't think it will cut through. It's not like it happened at a time when people were unable to hold the hands of their loved ones during their final terrifying moments on earth. I mean, it's exactly like that, but I think you have to frame it against the PM's superb job of handling the pandemic, always making decisions based on whatever he thought would make him most popular in a given moment. Under those circumstances, if he wants to drink a bottle of Bacardi and listen to Abba with his daughter's, sorry, girlfriend's friends after another gruelling three-hour day, who are we to object?

Friday, 3 December 2021

Texted Jodie to comment on the remarkable coincidence of this party story coming out so soon after I told it to her. I also apologised for my behaviour last weekend, admitting that I should have cleared it with her before inviting the strippers up to our room.

She replied saying she hasn't forgiven me, but gave me a glimmer of hope when she said that she did miss our chats about sensitive government business.

Saturday, 4 December 2021

The party story is still doing the rounds, but as I said to Matt Hancock during *Rocket League*, the most important thing is that it was a year ago. People are too fatigued by the things we're doing on a weekly basis to get upset about stuff that happened last year. The second rule of politics my mentor Neil Hamilton taught me is: 'If you give a man a bit of corruption he is annoyed for an hour. If you barrage him with endless corruption he'll become too exhausted to care.'

Sunday, 5 December 2021

Went to the Imperial War Museum with Nadine Dorries to look at tanks and asked her what she thinks I should do about Jodie. She offered to have a word.

Afterwards, in the gift shop, we spotted some rainbow erasers between the Dunkirk tea towels and Somme fridge magnets. 'People are sick and tired of having the National Trust's woke agenda rammed down their throats,' Nads screamed at the Saturday girl on the till.

It felt a bit weird leaving a sixteen-year-old sobbing, 'This isn't the National Trust,' so I told Nads I'd catch her up and bought the rubber to try and cheer the girl up. It didn't work, so I called her an ungrateful cow and left.

Monday, 6 December 2021

Leaked today: some footage of Allegra Stratton in the £2-million-Russian-money-funded briefing room we never use. She was having a mock press conference with her horsey mates about a hypothetical Christmas party that never happened.

How a gaggle of over-promoted graduates laughing about parties at a time when lockdown was driving people to suicide will pan out is anyone's guess.

Tuesday, 7 December 2021

Got a call from Jodie. Apparently, Nadine had threatened to nail her to the wall of Chozen Noodle with her own teeth unless she came on another date with me.

'Sorry, I must have misunderstood what Nadine meant by "having a word".'

'You asked her to do it?'

'No. Well, yes. But not like that.'

'You're unbelievable.'

'And?'

'And what?'

'And will you come on another date with me?'

She hung up. It was a setback. But I was also secretly touched the Fiat 500 Führer would go to such lengths for me.

Wednesday, 8 December 2021

The Defend the Indefensible WhatsApp group was strikingly quiet today. Not even Kwasi 'human shield' Kwarteng was willing to humiliate himself on the breakfast rounds. I volunteered to go out and tell Kay Burley that black is white, Dan Walker that up is down, and Adil Ray that Boris tells the truth; but I was instructed by CCHQ that there were no circumstances under which I would be allowed to speak to the media.

Boris made a solemn statement at PMQs, saying that he was as furious and shocked as the rest of us to watch his staff joking about an assumed Christmas party that they didn't go to. Then he turned the guns on Labour, accusing them of playing party politics with the pandemic, rather than just partying during it. I watched our benches with interest. Some of my colleagues were looking uneasy, and when the wind changes, which it always does, I don't want to find myself on the wrong side of the next leader.

Afterwards, I was in the kitchen taking a bite out of somebody else's Red Leicester when I was distracted by the sound of weeping. It was Allegra, crying into her John West Light Lunch. I went over and consoled her by explaining that unlike the single mum on benefits she humiliated on *Newsnight*, she was a proper human who hadn't done anything wrong.

Thursday, 9 December 2021

Allegra has resigned. But that doesn't matter because Boris and Carrie have had another kid. Incredible timing considering the heat about this Christmas party business. They say you're never more than six feet from a rat in London, and Boris is never more than six months away from a pregnant woman.

Friday, 10 December 2021

Had an arms meeting with some of the Saudis I met shooting. To show the delegation the more evocative side of Britain, I got Portillo to hire us a room at the Wyndham Sevenoaks Days Inn.

I arrived early after a good run on the A23 and sat down in reception with an *Express*. I was reading a superb article by Carole Malone about how Chris Whitty should be sacked because she'd only had a mild bout of Covid, when I saw a woman who looked just like Thérèse Coffey checking in. I shook my head and returned to Carole's effortless prose.

Even odder than that, thirty minutes later, I saw Gavin Williamson checking out, looking to all intents and purposes like he'd just done a triathlon.

I was just about to call over and ask what on earth he'd

been up to when I got tapped on the shoulder by one of four gentlemen in traditional Saudi ghutra and shades.

'Mr Secret Tory?'

'Imran. I didn't recognise you without your tweed.'

'And I didn't recognise you without your body armour, Mr Tory.' He turned to his friends. 'Mr Secret Tory wears Kevlar when he is shooting these fat English gaming birds. I am telling Mr Tory, these grouse, they are not Mossad.'

They roared with laughter, so I pretended to find it funny too.

'Pork scratching?' I said, offering around a bag of Mr Porky's, which they all declined.

A battered Vauxhall Astra pulled into the car park.

'Looks like the MoD have arrived. Right, let's do an arms deal.'

It had seemed prudent at the time to ask Portillo to book us a budget single room, but as Mohammed bin Salman, Imran Said, General Sir Bernard Fairfax, their respective entourages and a security detail squeezed in, it did feel a bit cramped.

But needs must. I got out the Joburg Munitions Enterprises Winter Collection catalogue and began my presentation. Mr Bin Salman, perched on a sink in the corner of the room, interrupted almost immediately.

'What is this?' he asked.

'A Heckler & Koch G36.'

'No, that this catalogue is balanced on?'

'Oh. A Corby trouser press. For getting a crease in your trousers.'

'I see.'

'Although you don't wear trousers, do you? Might be good for your ghutra?'

He looked at the others and they all made approving nods.

It went very well really. I sold five thousand machine guns, four F15s, ten thousand anti-personnel mines and a trouser press.

After some firm handshakes and a sinister joke about chopping mine off if I let them down, we left.

Saturday, 11 December 2021

Olly Dowden sent me up to Shropshire North to do some door knocking for the by-election caused by Owen Paterson's resignation. I got Portillo and Everton to come and help.

We started in Market Drayton, and after a couple of innocuous streets came across a pair of furtive men loitering around a urine-drenched phone box. The older man was inside it, tilting his head against the little black ledge where you used to put your change.

'What you up to, Mike?' I shouted across the road as the querulous Minister for Levelling Up, Michael Gove, emerged and handed his SPAD a rolled-up note.

'Winning votes,' he said, his glasses completely steamed up. 'You?'

'Same. Dowden obviously wanted the big hitters here,' I said nonchalantly. His aide re-emerged.

'How was that?' asked Michael, giving his handsome young assistant a firm pat on the bottom.

'Better now.'

Michael sniffed hard and seemed to stand a foot taller. He pushed his arms out to the sides, thumped his chest and said, 'OK, let's fucking level up,' before accosting a dog walker and shouting, 'Oi, what do you think about trickle-down economics?'

I nudged Portillo.

'That's how you do it, my boy.'

It was a long day. A typical exchange with a prospective Tory voter might go something like this:

'May I ask who you are voting for in the by-election, madam?'

'Who's the Conservative candidate?'

'I don't know. Portillo, who is the Conservative candi-date?'

'Neil Shastri-Hurst.'

'Will he get rid of those Travellers?'

'Er, I expect so.'

'Yes, then, as long as there's nothing good on telly that day.'

'Thank you, madam.'

We avoided the houses of people with organised-looking recycling systems to save time, but when we did encounter a non-Tory, a typical exchange might go something like this:

'Good afternoon, madam.'

'Oh, God. You're not a Tory, are you? Are you a Tory?'

'Yes, as a matter of fact I am.'

'What do you want?'

'May I ask if you have ever voted Conservative?'

'Yes.'

'Excellent.'

'No. You may ask me if I've ever voted Conservative.'

'Oh. Have you ever voted Conservative?'

'No.'

'May I ask why not?'

'Because you're a party of lying, cheating, embezzling, grifting, race-to-the-bottoming bastards who have barraged us with such a tsunami of self-interested incompetence that three-quarters of it has gone completely unnoticed. You are the party of the Monday Club, you have members who are openly misogynistic, homophobic, racist, antisemitic and Islamophobic, you're up to your necks in Russian money and favours, and with the current crop of chronically unskilled MPs and sycophantic ministers, you are dragging political discourse in this country down into the Mariana Trench of slurry.'

'Right ...'

'No, I haven't finished. You bleat from your subsidised canteens that you need second jobs because your £84,000 is not enough to get by on, while begrudging society's most vulnerable children their lunch, and that makes sense in your empathy-free vacuums because you think people with money have earned it, while single mums, disabled people and substance misusers who've never been given a first, second or, in your boss's case, three-hundredth chance, just aren't trying hard enough. I think your outlook is indicative of the laziest kind of conniving dogma. I'm only sad that I don't believe in fate because the infernal comeuppance your cowardly country-wrecking cohort deserve might never happen.'

'Right …'

'No, I still haven't finished. That said, with leaders in charge of the calibre of Truss, Kwarteng and Coffey, a *Mad Max*-style apocalypse that results in your blood-eagled corpses being dragged around College Green on dirt bikes by gangs of marauding anti-vaxxers in nappies isn't too far beyond the realms of possibility.'

'And does that mean you will or won't be voting for us today?'

'Get off my flower bed.'

Sunday, 12 December 2021

Olly phoned to tell me that the CCHQ switchboard had lit up with calls from members of the Shropshire faithful concerned that 'someone like Everton' was walking around sporting a blue rosette. He also said that the campaign wasn't going very well, and he was thinking of bringing Gary Barlow on board and asked if I could go and sound him out. Apparently, he wants to become an MP and he thinks this would be a great opportunity for him to practise his campaigning.

Monday, 13 December 2021

I met with Gary in Gail's Bakery, Kensington. He was going incognito in a 1994 Take That world tour tee-shirt.

'Hi, I'm Secret Tory.'

He peered at me over the top of his aviators.

'I'm Gary Barlow. I'm incognito. I need to vet you before I invite you into my house.'

He called over to the till: 'Is that coffee for Mr Barlow ready yet?'

'Two minutes, Gary.'

'Right, first things first, you haven't asked Robbie Williams or any of the others to do this have you?'

'No.'

'Great, consider yourself vetted. Let's go to Beethoven Villas.'

He took me to his modest eighteen-bed town house, sat down at one of three grand pianos and began playing 'Knees up Mother Brown'.

'Mother Brown,' I said. 'You probably can't say that any more.'

'Knees up, knees up, knees up – exactly, Secret Tory – knees up, knees up Mother Brown.' He stopped and looked at me as if he'd just had a wonderful idea. 'Fancy some arrers?'

'Sure.'

We went down into his basement, where he had built an exact replica of the Lakeside Country Club, Frimley Green.

'Eighteen months of earth-shifting lorries. The Lloyd Webbers hated it.'

'I can imagine. Look at this place.'

'I get Little Richard Ashdown to come down and MC for me. Although he doesn't like it because Sol Campbell, who I play with, is rubbish and it takes forever.'

'Olly tells me you're keen to become an MP. Do you think we could have a party in here next time there's a lockdown?'

'I don't see why not. It's time to put a bit back, Secret. And halve my tax liability.'

'Well, Gary, that's why I'm here. How would you like to practise your front-line campaigning? CCHQ were wondering if you'd like to come and help in the Shropshire North by-election.'

'Can you arrange for me to meet Kwasi Kwarteng?'

'Er, yes.'

'Then I'll do it.'

Tuesday, 14 December 2021

Boris has introduced Covid Plan B – work from home but go to your Christmas party. So I followed his advice to the letter and spent the afternoon playing *Command & Conquer*, which is exactly what I'd been planning on doing at work.

But then Steve Baker called another one of his bloody Covid Research Group meetings and we all had to go back in.

'Who are we to believe? Scientists, who have decided that the universe is 13.8 billion years old? Or the Bible, which clearly states it is 6.5 thousand? They can't both be right. And I don't know about you, but I'd trust the word of a stout English yeoman like Jesus over these lefty lab coats any day of the week. Now, I would like to hand you over to Mark Harper, my fellow witness to the majesty of God on the A40 corridor.'

He passed him the ceremonial CRG speaking swede and Mark began a riveting PowerPoint on all the science the mainstream media have been withholding.

There was a graph that had patriotism on its X axis and Covid immunity on the Y, revealing that the more jingoistic you are, the less namby-pamby state interference you need; a pie-chart showing that the less you test for Covid, the less of it you find; and a scatter graph highlighting the correlation between fewer restrictions and more money in donors' pockets.

We sat in a stunned silence. How have the lamestream media dared to keep this sort of stuff hidden from us?

Des Swayne got Mark to throw him the speaking swede.

'And another thing. Isn't it convenient that this "killer virus" is invisible to the man in the street? They're expecting us to believe something exists that nobody has ever even seen. If they can put a man on the moon—'

'Debatable,' said John Redwood.

'Not without the swede, John', said Steve.

'You don't have it either,' John replied.

'That's not the point,' said Steve.

Des continued: 'If they can put a man on the moon—'

John raised his hand, Des threw him the swede.

'Debatable.'

John threw it back.

'Fuck's sake, Redders. I've lost my train of thought,' said Des, tossing the swede up and down to jog his memory before slamming it into the table. 'Look, basically what I'm saying is, if you gave me five minutes bareknuckle with Covid, one on one, I could deck it and end the pandemic on the spot.'

We banged our desks.

Afterwards, Andrew Bridgen confided: 'I'll level with you, Secret. I didn't understand any of it.'

'Not even the graphs?'

'Especially not the graphs.'

'If anyone asks, just say that Omicron is a cold, and if any burnt-out NHS staff complain that we're unnecessarily pushing their hospitals to breaking point, tell them we're building forty new ones to alleviate the strain. And if they don't like that then tell them they should just go and retrain in cyber.'

'Great. I'm on Sky in fifteen, I'll say that.'

Wednesday, 15 December 2021

Shropshire North is in the balance. I dropped everything to go back up there ASAP. I sat outside Portillo's therapy session with my hand on the horn of the Overfinch until he emerged, then told him he needed to drive me up the M5.

He was uncommunicative for most of the journey (something to do with this sort of thing being the reason he's in therapy in the first place), and anyway he drove so slowly that I had to make him pull over at Corley North so I could take over.

We met up with the campaign team in a Pets at Home car park. On the other side of the road, coming out of a Tesco Express, were Ed Miliband and Angela Rayner eating meal deals.

'They're eating baked crisps,' shrieked Thérèse Coffey. 'Look, Gavin, they eat baked.'

'Can't handle blokes' crisps, Ed?' shouted Dom Raab.

'What are blokes' crisps, Dom?' Ed returned over the traffic.

'Oh, I don't know …' He left a decent pause. 'McCoy's!'

We all cheered.

'Miliband, you fockin' cont!' screamed Nadine.

'Shall I go and tamper with the brakes on Starmer's Micra?' Priti asked quietly.

'No, I don't think we need to do that,' Olly replied.

Jess Phillips emerged from the automatic doors with a £2.99 sushi box and immediately got into the spirit of things.

'All right, Boris, do your mistresses know you're here?'

'Like I'd tell a fishwife like you!'

From the comfort of his luxury yacht, Geoffrey Cox had been mimicking Ed by saying, 'Hell yeth, I'm tough enough', through his aide's tablet, but the integrated speaker wasn't up to much and nobody could hear him.

'I'll handle this Geoff,' said Penny Mordaunt to the tablet, who then shouted at Ed, 'Hell yeth, I'm tough enough.'

'I am tough enough actually,' replied Ed.

Gary flew across the street and began to berate him.

'You. Miliband. Nobody talks to Penny Mordaunt like that.'

Penny looked smugly at Nadine.

'With your socialism and your brother and your rubbish sandwich-eating skills, it would have been chaos with you. Thank God the public voted for twelve years of corruption-free stability with the Tories.'

'Look, Gary, I'm thorry you feel like that,' said Ed. 'Perhapth we thould—'

'Fuck off. How many press-ups can you do?'

'Gary, I'd like to think that ath adultth we can thettle our differences without rethorting to dithplayth of phythical thtrength ...'

'Six, seven, eight.' Gary was already underway, pressing-up on a manhole cover.

'Gary, I'm not thure thith ith the right way to ...'

A bus queue, a couple with a puppy and a man with a fish tank migrated over to see what the ruling elite and the crooner who wrote 'A Million Love Songs' were up to.

'... fifteen, sixteen, seventeen ...'

Whether it was Nadine calling him a 'scab' or Raab masticating a McCoy in his face that tipped him over the edge, we'll never know, but there was a collective gasp when Miliband suddenly ripped off his shirt to reveal deltoids like boulders, pecs like anvils and a torso with more definition than the dictionary, and leapt into a series of double-handclap-at-the-top press-ups beside Gary, who had already collapsed on the pavement.

Ed was relentless, reaching a hundred inside sixty seconds before springing back to his feet and screaming at the prostrate figure, 'You like that, Gary? You like that? You want some more, you shit Jason Orange?'

Thérèse and I dragged Gary into the safety of her Dacia while Penny and Nadine fought over cleaning him up, and over the sound of the doughy singer-songwriter sacking his personal trainer, Ed jumped onto the bonnet, thumped his chest and thundered, 'Hell, yeth, I'm tough enough,' at the gloomy Shropshire sky.

Thursday, 16 December 2021

Last day of campaigning, so Portillo, Neil Shastri-Hurst, Gary Barlow, Michael Gove and I headed out door-knocking after a leisurely lunch.

In one cul-de-sac of pensioner-ridden bungalows we found a property defended by gnomes and a lot of Sellotaped biro messages about unsolicited pizza menus.

'Good afternoon,' said a large silver-haired man with glasses. 'Is this important? We were watching the bowls.'

'Hello, yes it is. I'm Neil Shastri-Hurst, your Conservative candidate in the by-election tomorrow. I was wondering if I could count—'

A revitalised Gary pushed him out of the way. 'I'll handle this, Derek.'

'Neil.'

'Whatever. Hello, I'm Gary Barlow, Neil's boss. Can we count on your vote when the phonelines open tomorrow?'

'Gary Barlow … Gary Barlow, that rings a bell.'

Gary gave us a knowing look.

'I love your songs, especially that "Angels" one, and I've voted Tory all my life, but a girl from the Lib Dems came here earlier, and you know what? She really cut through.'

'So you're saying you want your street filling up with foreigners?'

'Er …'

Before the householder could formulate an answer, Michael Gove pushed through our huddle.

'Please, I need to use your toilet.'

'Mavis, is it all right if Michael Gove comes in to use the lav?'

Mavis didn't answer.

'Er, yes, sure, Michael. Go straight ahead.'

Mike sprinted into the loo and slammed the door, at which point Mavis emerged.

'John, what's all this hullaballoo?'

'It's Tories, Mavis. They were just asking if it was OK if Michael Gove uses the downstairs loo.'

'John, no!' gasped Mavis. 'It's still blocked from Joyce visiting earlier. Send him upstairs.'

She froze as sounds emanated from behind the thin balsa door: 'Oh no,' followed by a 'fft, fft, fft' like a helicopter crashing, an, 'Ahhhh', two more 'fft, ffts', an, 'Oh, thank goodness', and another, 'Ahhhh'.

I knew we needed to regain the initiative.

'John, Mavis, hi. I'm Secret Tory. Is there anything we could say today that would make you change your mind?'

But before either could answer, my phone rang.

'Yes? Calm down, mate. Yes. Yes. OK.' I covered the receiver. 'I've got Michael on the phone. He was wondering if you had any lavatory paper?'

'White or pink?' asked Mavis.

'He's the Minister for Levelling Up, Mavis. Get the pink,' said John.

Mavis shuffled over to the cupboard under the stairs.

'There's nothing stopping you doing this, John, you know. It's always in the same place.'

'Is it?'

She looked at the rest of us. 'Fifty-two years. Fifty-two years we've been married. It's always been in the same place.'

'Men,' tutted Gary while shaking his head. Mavis looked at him curiously.

'The householder is coming, Michael. Hold fire.'

Mavis knocked, the door slid sideways and a skinny arm shot out and withdrew the roll.

'Thank you,' peeped Michael.

'So. The by-election. Can I count on your vote?' asked Neil. John looked at his wife, then at the toilet door. Then back at us.

'Erm, no, I don't think so.' He looked at Gary. 'But as you're here, do you think we could get an autograph for our daughter, please?'

'Why don't you fuck off?' replied Gary.

'OK, we'll be off now, thank you very much,' said Portillo.

'Michael?' I called to the door.

'Five minutes.'

I turned back to the householders.

'Would it be OK if we left Michael Gove here for five minutes?'

'Er, yes, that should be fine,' said John.

It was a long afternoon, and the doorsteps were tough. But I still think we can win it.

Friday, 17 December 2021

We have lost Shropshire North with one of the biggest swings in post-war history. The message is clear: Owen Paterson shouldn't have resigned.

Saturday, 18 December 2021

A picture has emerged of Boris and nineteen of his core team, including Carrie, having a work meeting in the garden of Number Ten last May.

The usual suspects – Deborah Meaden, Hugh Grant, my binman – were all grumbling about it. I'm so bloody bored of these self-righteous metropolitans saying they were burying their soulmates alone. If they'd cared that much about them then they would have broken the rules like the rest of us.

Sunday, 19 December 2021

Got Chris Chope in CRG Secret Santa. Struggling for ideas.

Monday, 20 December 2021

David Frost has resigned as Brexit minister. Someone has leaked screenshots from our Clean Global Brexit WhatsApp chat. Geoffrey Clifton-Brown wrote: 'Frost is a hero and 100 per cent right, this is a hammer blow to the PM. He desperately needs a really strong adviser at No. 10 who he can trust.'

Nadine replied, 'The hero is the Prime Minister who delivered Brexit.'

Then Steve Baker kicked her out of the group. He has become unpredictable since he said Moses appeared to him in the dogging layby on the A355 Beaconsfield to Amersham.

Tuesday, 21 December 2021

Convinced Jodie to come Christmas shopping with me, by doing it at Clacket Lane and visiting her during her lunch break.

'So I've got a really tricky Secret Santa.'

'Right.'

'What would you get a man in his seventies who has objected to legislation banning upskirting, giving courts increased protective power over girls at risk of FGM, pardoning Alan Turing, protecting poor countries from vulture funds, preventing wild animals being used in circus performances, prohibiting revenge evictions from vexatious landlords and, only last month, the motion from the Select Committee on Standards that would have passed the report regarding the rules breached by Owen Paterson?'

'Who the hell would be so insufferably obnoxious as to do all that?'

'Chris Chope. He's actually very principled; he only does it when he's concerned legislation hasn't had sufficient scrutiny.'

'Does he do it for all legislation?'

'No, he doesn't do it for bills put forward by his mates.'

'Then I wouldn't get him anything. He sounds like a piece of shit.'

Wednesday, 22 December 2021

Geoffrey Cox has finally got round to looking at that fine I got for parking in a Westminster disabled bay. His aide held the tablet while Geoff sat on a pedalo sipping a piña colada. He agreed to sort it for two grand, half his usual rate. I gave the aide my card. She put it in a reader and entered my PIN.

'How on earth do you know my PIN?' I asked.

'All Tory MP's pins are 1922.'

'Two grand,' I sighed. I'd only just got paid two grand by Joburg Munitions Systems.

'How much was the fine?'

'Hundred and eighty quid.'

She looked at me sympathetically.

'Exactly,' I said. 'The sooner MPs are allowed to take second jobs, the better.'

Thursday, 23 December 2021

I had a flash of inspiration for Chris Chope's Secret Santa and bought him a small digital camera on a stick that he can carry around discreetly on public transport. We did the exchange in Westminster Hall this morning. Des Swayne was Santa, wringing a lot of mileage about 'rummaging around in his sack' as he distributed the gifts. Mine was an interesting shape. I took it home with interest.

Friday, 24 December 2021

Christmas Eve. Had a lovely day observing all my little traditions: mince pies, whisky and carrots for Santa and the reindeer, watching *Saw III*.

Saturday, 25 December 2021

I don't care if you're five and waking up to your drunk father quoting Enoch Powell and kicking the dog down the stairs, or fifty-five and waking up in a five-bed detached with nobody else in it because you're incapable of forging meaningful relationships – the excitement of Christmas Day never wears off.

I rushed downstairs to see if he'd been. Deep down I knew. But there's always a chance, and certainly, there's more evidence for Santa than there is for man-made climate change. But it didn't matter. Because when I went to the front door to dispose of the overnight dogshit postings, I was stopped in my tracks. Gentle snowflakes were falling – snowflakes that wouldn't exist if the planet was getting hotter.

Even though she's the sort of calculating bitch who can get a court to agree that her ex-husband is a 'grasping bastard', Portillo prefers Christmas at his mum's. But just as I opened the door he pulled up on his bicycle and threw a little snowball at me.

'Happy Christmas, Dad.'

'You little tyke,' I shouted back, launching a bagged dogshit back at him. 'Can you stay for long?'

'Not really. I'm going to have to go home and get changed now.'

We did presents on the doorstep. I unwrapped his. A

laminated A5 card with all my logins and passwords for Parliament, the constituency, Twitter, LinkedIn etc.

'And this is for you, son,' I said, handing him an envelope.

'What is it? You don't usually get me anything.'

'Open it and see,' I said mischievously.

'A speeding ticket from the drive up to Shropshire?' He studied it further. 'But this is from the M6 toll when you were driving.'

'I know, but I've got a clean licence and I want to keep it that way. So I put your name down.'

'Dad, I've already got nine points from all the other tickets of yours I've taken. This will get me banned.'

'Well, you should have thought about that before accepting the others then shouldn't you? Happy Christmas though.'

After he'd gone, and in honour of my own father, I loaded 'Rivers of Blood' up on YouTube and drank Santa's whisky.

Then I opened my presents. I got a Sports Direct 'Sovereign-tee' tee-shirt from Des Swayne (I know for a fact he has 500 of these in his garage), another knitted Michael Caine doll from Elsie and Lucy, a PPE contract to supply hi-spec facemasks from Matt Hancock, a signed copy from Mark Francois of his self-published autobiography *Spartan Victory*, a book about mindfulness from Sir Edward Leigh, and an M240B machine gun from Mick Miller. My Secret Santa was the most intriguing, though: a long-range paparazzi-style shot of my arms meeting with the Saudis at that hotel in Essex with the caption 'I know what you did last winter …'

What a lovely idea, a thoughtful colleague celebrating my industrious extra-parliamentary activities with a picture.

At eleven the Burkes, in matching organic angora pullovers, knocked on the door and began singing 'We Wish You a Merry Christmas'. I took a few minutes to answer.

'Sorry, guys, I was just in the Aitken Suite.'

'The Aitken Suite?'

'Downstairs bog.'

I wiped my wet hands on my thighs and took one of the vegan mince pies they were offering. After a nudge from his wife, Mr Burke said, 'Secret, I know we haven't always seen eye to eye, but I, er we, we saw Portillo leaving earlier and we just wanted to come and say Happy Christmas and …' He hesitated. Mrs Burke nudged him again. He took a breath and gabbled, 'and say that if you're not doing anything later you'd be welcome to come over to ours for Christmas dinner.'

'With you lot? No way. I'm not lonely, I've got loads on.'

Three and a half hours later I popped on my jacket and sauntered over to their house, eyeballing the infuriating bamboo windchimes as I went. Mrs Burke answered the door.

'Yes, interesting thing, turns out an M&S turkey for one cooks quite quickly and mine has become comprehensively burnt. I don't suppose that offer of Christmas dinner still stands?'

She didn't say anything.

'I mean, I presume it does because it would be very odd to rescind it after three hours.'

I walked in. The living room was warm, with greenery everywhere and the smell of chestnuts permeating the house. The children were playing a game called Holistic Operation in front of an eco-pellet fire and there were trays of nibbles everywhere.

'Ah, Secret, welcome to our humble abode,' said Mr Burke, looking at his wife with weird eyes. 'Please, make yourself at home.'

I sat down, apologised to the children for standing on their new game and inhaled a bowl of salted cashews.

It was all right really. Apart from the non-denominational grace, a heated debate about immigration, a repellent nut roast and the children being inconsolable because I'd destroyed their Christmas present.

At five, not fancying another round of Nobel Peace Prize Charades, I made my excuses, apologised for not contributing any nibbles, and made my way home to crisps, nuts, pickled eggs, a six-pack of Castlemaine and *Mrs Brown's Boys*.

Sunday, 26 December 2021

Just after midnight I was woken on the sofa by howling. And after a few moments I realised that it wasn't the sound I usually make during my recurring nightmare about being trapped in a Crouch End coffee shop with Anna Soubry. This was coming from the garden. I went to the back door.

There in the snow, tethered to my eight-foot flagpole, sat a pair of Labrador puppies. I looked around. There was no one to be seen. Just a single pair of footprints in the snow.

I bloody knew it. Santa does exist! In your face climate change.

I fell on them, and they nuzzled and licked my face in return. It was festive delight, my lonely house suddenly filled with puppyish joy and excitement. But I was pretty tired so after twenty seconds I shoved them in the cupboard under the stairs and went back to bed.

Thirteen hours later, the point at which I could no longer cope with their howling, I got up, fed them a pickled egg each, and named them Stuffy and Butcher, after Hugh Dowding and Bomber Harris.

Then I tethered them to a Lockheed Martin lanyard and we went for a stroll, which, apart from two punctured tyres on a little girl's new BMX, went remarkably well. We wandered down to the canal where I like to go fly-tipping, and I was somewhat taken aback to see Steve Baker in a reindeer mask waving off a hatchback full of climate-science deniers. I knew it was Steve because his rimless bifocals were visible either side of his mask, and I knew they were climate-science deniers because they had Global Warming Policy Forum written on the side of their Vauxhall Nova.

'Happy Christmas, Steve!' I shouted as he fumbled for the keys of his Skoda Octavia. He seemed unable to hear me.

'Happy Christmas, Steve!' I repeated, louder this time. He still didn't hear me, but then Stuffy slipped his lead, ran over and began worrying his clammy jogging bottoms, and Steve dropped a wad of cash on the floor. 'Sorry about that, Steve. Present from Santa,' I said as I tried to stop Stuffy humping his leg.

'I'm not Steve,' replied Steve, getting into his car.

'OK, Steve.'

He turned the ignition.

'See you at CRG Wednesday week, Steve.'

The Skoda began rolling away, then stopped: 'It's Thursday this month.'

Monday, 27 December 2021

Another wonderful day with the puppies, capped off by Chris Chope texting to say he'd spent an absorbing day on the Circle Line and was absolutely thrilled with the definition on his new camera.

Tuesday, 28 December 2021

My little Christmas miracle has come to an end. I was curled up watching *Escape to Victory* with the boys when I got a text from John Redwood.

'Did you get the dogs?'

'What?'

'The Dogs. Two Labradors.'

'Oh, right. Yes.'

'Someone tipped off the police about my illegal puppy farm so I had to hide them and lie low for a bit. I left two tied to the flag in your garden.'

'Oh, yes. I thought that was you.'

'Good. I need them back, they're for Sarah Vine. I'll be over later. And if anyone from the RSPCA comes snooping around and asking questions, you haven't seen me.'

He arrived an hour later looking very much like he'd been lying low for a few days. It was hard to say goodbye to Stuffy and Butcher, but knowing that a generous soul like Sarah was going to be caring for them gave me much solace.

Wednesday, 29 December 2021

It's that bit in between Christmas and New Year, when you don't know what on earth to do with yourself; like the rest of the year but with marginally better TV.

Thursday, 30 December 2021

Declined an invitation to a tarts and vicars party at Mike Fabricant's house on the grounds that Steve Barclay got chlamydia at the last one and claims he was fully clothed the whole time.

Friday, 31 December 2021

New Year's Eve. A day which brings back a lot of memories. In 1999, for example, I was so concerned about the Millennium Bug that I boarded up my house and applied for a gun licence, which was declined on the grounds of my utter unsuitability.

The Silicon Valley apocalypse never came to pass. But I didn't find that out for several days because I was bunkered down playing *Command & Conquer: Red Alert* while imagining the carnage outside: traffic lights firing lasers, planes falling from the sky and the sort of people who hover in supermarket reductions areas fulfilling the warning signs they've been giving off for years by rampaging across town centres nationwide.

After five days, with the frozen food finished, my hands covered in cuts because I'd lost the tin opener and was opening cans with my cheese knife, and Buckingham Palace comprehensively captured by Russian forces in *Command &*

Conquer, I determined to make a break for the nearest burnt-out Londis. I wrenched the plasterboard off my new UPVC windows and climbed out, my eyes struggling to adjust to the natural light.

'Hello, Secret Tory.'

'Who said that?'

'Mrs Burke.'

'Oh. You. What are our new robot overlords like?'

'What?'

'The Millennium Bug. What's happened? Has society collapsed? Are you some sort of war chief now?'

'No. I'm off to yoga.'

'Right.'

'We were wondering why we hadn't seen you. Have you been hiding?'

'Yes. No,' I said, trying to look as though I hadn't been sitting out judgement day in a sealed Barratt new build.

I took off the night-vision goggles I was wearing and realised that the sunlight wasn't the reason I couldn't see; it was because they didn't work.

'Why have you got cuts all over your hands?'

'No reason. So you're telling me everything is fine?'

'Well, Cherie Blair got fined for not having a valid train ticket between Blackfriars and Luton yesterday, but other than that, things have been pretty normal.'

I found myself filling with rage, not only at the nerds, with their talking paperclip and non-existent Armageddon, but at a Labour regime so entitled that Cherie Blair seemed to think she could ride on privatised public transport gratis.

When I got home and found a note from my wife saying this was no way to live and she and Portillo were leaving me, I knew I could never rest until I'd crushed Cool Britannia. So I picked up the phone and applied to become a Tory MP.

I had a quieter one this year, four Carlings and a strudel in front of *True Lies*.

January 2022

Saturday, 1 January 2022

Woken by noises again, this time in the living room. Went down to find Stephen Crabb and Matt Hancock watching Adam Sandler films with a wrap of bash.

'I let myself in, I've still got a key,' explained Stephen.

'Aren't you supposed to be in Pembrokeshire?'

'She's kicked me out again.'

He turned to Hancock and they did a fist-bump hand-slap routine which involved taking it in turns to say:

'Fathers …'

'For …'

'Justice.'

Sunday, 2 January 2022

Spent the day watching films with the boys. But by four, when Stephen had blocked the Aitken Suite for a second time and they were suggesting getting started on *Zulu*, I lied and told them that Priti was on her way over. They were off the sofa and on their way back to their bedsits quicker than you can say, 'Babe, I'm so sorry. I love you so much. It was a stupid mistake; I promise I'll never do it again.'

Monday, 3 January 2022

Went into work but forgot it was a bank holiday and Parliament was shut. Nadine had done the same thing. She was standing at the end of Downing Street beneath a Lambert & Butler umbrella sketching a picture of Boris on the back of DCMS briefing documents. It was a very good likeness, although since I've never seen him in Speedos I don't know if he's got a Herculean frame and tattoo of Nadine or not.

Tuesday, 4 January 2022

First day back proper. The PM gave a rousing assembly saying that Partygate was behind us and this term we were going to be getting on with the job in hand of turbocharging the economy, building back better and levelling up Britain. We all cheered.

He then handed over to Matt Hancock, who read from a piece of paper shaking in his hands.

'Partygate might be behind us, but Fridgegate is …' He paused to retch. 'Is ahead of us.'

He appeared to gulp something down.

'And when I lay my hands on whoever is pilfering their colleagues' ready meals from the fridge, I'll be calling the police …' He turned over his quivering piece of paper. 'To retrieve the asphyxiated corpse of an MP in a pair of suspenders with an orange stuck in their mouth,' he finished, unconvincingly.

'Don't threaten Fabricant without any evidence,' boomed Boris.

It was a great gag and had everyone laughing, apart from Steve Baker who stood silently at the back, taking notes.

Wednesday, 5 January 2022

Despite yesterday's reassurances, Partygate is still dominating the headlines. Tom Tugendhat, Rishi Sunak and Liz Truss have all been posting carefully worded tweets saying they support the boss without actually saying it. This can only mean one thing: leadership manoeuvres.

Thursday, 6 January 2022

The Colston Four, the people who knocked over that statue of the slaver Edward Colston, have been exonerated. It's disgusting. Colston was a product of his time. Nobody knew slavery was wrong in the seventeenth century. Apart from the slaves. And all the other contemporary sources who objected. And Shakespeare. And the Saxon bishop Wulfstan who railed against it from the same docks into which Colston's statue was pushed, four centuries before Colston was born. But other than that, nobody knew it was wrong.

Friday, 7 January 2022

Watched *Seven* and realised I'm sick of watching life pass me by, so I texted Jodie and told her I had some gossip. It worked. We're going out for lunch tomorrow.

Saturday, 8 January 2022

I could tell this date was going to be make or break by the way Jodie texted:

'Don't get your hopes up.'

So I went all in and took her to the most romantic place I know: Beaconsfield Services.

With its extensive food court, triple-banked fruit-machine studio and a Wetherspoons for when you need a pint in the middle of a drive to Wales, it is, in my humble opinion, the best service station in the UK.

I was waxing lyrically about this to Jodie, with reference to Peterborough Extra, Wetherby Roadchef and the next-generation multi-floored facility at Cobham, as we waited for onion rings and John Smith's from the table-service app.

'Can we talk about something else please? I'm sick to death of service stations, I've spent the last ten years working in them.'

'Don't interrupt. What was I saying? Ah yes, the two-hourly urinal cleans at Wetherby Roadchef – they don't miss a drop.'

A barwoman brought our John Smith's. I pointed to them.

'See, I don't forget.'

'I drink Tetley's.'

'Right,' I said irritably. 'I'll get you another.'

'No, no, it's fine. So, you said you had some more gossip. Tell me, what do you know about all these lockdown parties? Did …'

I shuffled in my plastic seat and groaned.

'What's wrong?'

'My Plymouths.'

'What?'

'They've been playing up all week.'

She was blank. I nodded down.

'Plymouth Argyles. Piles.'

I put my Barbour jacket over her shoulders.

'Why are you doing that?'

'Because you just shivered.'

'It wasn't because I'm cold.'

I lifted a buttock off my chair. 'Good. The chilly weather plays havoc with these guys.'

She took a breath. 'So, come on, what's been going on at work? Any more "mad" stories?'

'Not really. Everyone is banging on about the Christmas parties, but they were nothing really compared with the booze-ups we had during the first lockdown. Wine-time Fridays.'

She sat up. 'What?'

'Oh, you know, forty-people booze-ups, wine on the walls, BYOB garden parties, suitcase runs to Tesco to stock up, Boris doing lines of cocaine off Hansard. Stuff like that. It was funny, because one minute Oliver Dowden would be on the BBC telling everyone to stay indoors, and the next we're getting on one in the Rose Garden.'

'I don't believe you.'

'Yes way.'

'Prove it,' she said, putting a hand on my knee. At last, after all this time, she was succumbing to my charms.

'OK, hang on a minute.' I scrolled through my phone. 'There you go. Look, an email invite sent round by the PM's Principal Private Secretary, Martin Reynolds.'

She squinted at the screen. 'I haven't got my glasses. Can you forward it to me?'

'I didn't know you wear glasses?'

'Yeah, big time.'

'Sent. Another pint?'

'Why not?'

I don't think the date could have gone any better. I spoke at length about the rudderless party culture at Downing Street and she hung off my every word. It was magic. I made my move.

'Well, there's an online poker tournament with Mike Fabricant and Ian Botham I need to be getting home to. Would you like to come back and watch?'

'Come to your house and watch you play online poker?'

'Yes. There's a Londis by the station; you could buy yourself some cans.'

'Er …'

'It'd be on a laptop, not a tablet. Texas hold 'em?'

'No, I think I'm OK Secret Tory. I've had a lovely time, but I'd like to stay here.'

'Here? Junction 2 of the M40? How will you get home?'

'I'll figure something out.'

'OK, well I'll call you. Perhaps we could do Cobham next time?'

'Sure.'

And then, dear reader, we had our first kiss. It wasn't as I'd imagined it – I leant in to kiss her, she ducked under the table and I kissed her scalp – but a kiss is still a kiss.

I skipped away like a giddy lad, wiping brunette hair and dandruff from my tongue. Love's young dream, well and truly alive in Beaconsfield Extra.

As a footnote, on the way out I saw Rachel Reeves and Pippa Crerar from the *Mirror* get up from a KFC-covered food-court table. I thought about saying hello, then remembered I hated them and bought a Ribena from the Cornwall Pasty Co. instead.

Sunday, 9 January 2022

I've written a template email for Portillo to reply to my disgruntled constituents about Partygate:

> Dear Disgruntled Constituent,
> During the lockdown Boris made the shrewd calculation that 170,000 corpses wouldn't make a fuss if he had a rave in his garden. What he didn't factor in was the mourners that the cadavers left behind. This is not his problem. It is yours. You should have broken the rules and gone and said goodbye properly. Never mind. One day your grief will pass, and you will be able to see that our response to the Covid pandemic was world-beating.
> Yours sincerely,
> Secret Tory

Monday, 10 January 2022

A huge day for Brexit. Ben Bradley has found an article in the *Daily Express* saying that our courgette trade with Morocco has increased by 800 per cent and is now worth over £500,000 a year. It's happening. Dividends are being reaped.

Tuesday, 11 January 2022

The story I told Jodie about Boris's chief of staff inviting a hundred people to a BYOB lockdown party at Number Ten has surfaced in the media. What are the chances? I texted her to comment on the odd coincidence and to reassure her that I knew it wasn't her because she respects me too much, but for some reason my phone said calls to this number were now barred.

Wednesday, 12 January 2022

In a bid to get away from the second-year uni vibe permeating Downing Street, the plan to save Boris's premiership has been called Operation Big Dog.

Subsequent to the discovery that he was at the party he said he wasn't at, he gave a heartfelt and succinct apology in the chamber, explaining that now he's been caught lying he truly understands how angry people are about him lying and that he had only joined the party for twenty-five minutes and, anyway, the rules he made stated that only two people could meet outside socially, so a gathering of thirty was within them.

It was compelling stuff, his face contorted in the manner of someone who'd spent the preceding two hours being coached to look recalcitrant, and I had no doubt in my mind that before us we had a man who desperately wanted to keep his job.

The idiot Starmer wasted his questions demanding to know why Boris thought the rules didn't apply to him, instead of asking something useful about freeports.

Afterwards, Boris was in the Stranger's Bar geeing up the Redwallers with his Hylda Baker impressions.

'Oh, is that the time? I really ought to get a second hand put on this watch. By the way, I haven't done anything wrong, you know. I'm bravely taking the blame for everyone else.'

I'm not sure they bought it. Their majorities are too small.

Thursday, 13 January 2022

The *Telegraph* has reported that Boris's staff had two parties the night before the funeral of Prince Philip, when our exemplar of duty Her Royal Highness the Queen sat alone.

I don't understand what the fuss is about. If you can't celebrate when you've limited deaths on your watch to a mere 170,000, when can you?

Friday, 14 January 2022

Just when he had the opportunity to put these Partygate stories to bed once and for all, someone in Boris's household caught Covid and he must now miss engagements for the rest of the week. He has some rotten luck: he was on holiday when that report about his handling of the pandemic came out, he was flying to Afghanistan during the vote on Heathrow and he got stuck in a fridge when breakfast TV wanted to talk to him about his oven-ready deal.

Saturday, 15 January 2022

Went for my traditional New Year sauna with Prince Andrew. He was a bit sad because the Queen had just stripped him of all his titles.

'Well, at least you'll be travelling lighter. You'll probably save a bit on your petrol too.'

'Well, yes, Secret Tory, you do always seem to find the bright side. I very much admire that. Indeed, I've recently become very interested in climate change. One of my New

Year's resolutions is to reduce my carbon footprint by not going to America any more.'

'You're so noble, Andy.'

'Indeed I am. And may I ask, Secret Tory, what are yours?'

'Well, there's this girl.'

His ears pricked up. 'Oh, yes?'

'I say girl, she's forty-three.'

He lost interest again.

'But I really like her. She's like nobody else I've ever met. But I don't know how to progress things.'

'Oh yes, well, that's very difficult. My first step would be getting her to sign an NDA.'

He suggested we go for a pizza in Woking afterwards, but I declined, citing a pre-existing repeat engagement with *The Rock* on Sky Action.

Sunday, 16 January 2022

Nadine did some good briefing against the BBC today. She's cutting £4 billion from their budget. Peter Bottomley and the rest of the liberal elite were moaning that the BBC does things like clear its schedules to offer comprehensive free education to every child in the country during lockdown, but those of us who are sick to death of having *Match of the Day*, *Line of Duty*, *The Antiques Roadshow* and David Attenborough rammed down our throats can finally see light at the end of the tunnel. People seem to think that because we're called Conservatives we like conserving things. But like public schools and James Cleverly, names are often deceptive.

Monday, 17 January 2022

Andrew Bridgen told *News at Ten* that he'd submitted a letter of no confidence in Boris. Every Tory WhatsApp group lit up immediately. None of us knew he could write.

Tuesday, 18 January 2022

Bury South MP Christian Wakeford was sobbing in a heap on the floor outside the kitchen today. He'd had a run-in with Mark Spencer and the Rodney to his chief whip Del Boy, Conor Burns.

I thought about asking if he was OK, but then I realised I really fancied a Subway Meatball Marinara, which was a coincidence because I could see that Christian had just abandoned a Subway Meatball Marinara on the counter.

I fled into meeting room eight with it, but when I sat down to eat I heard a noise coming from the store cupboard. Upon investigating, I was not as taken aback as I should have been to discover Matt Hancock smashing up some enamel NHS badges with a Ministry of Justice gavel.

'What are you doing, Matt?'

'Someone shared a video of me doing parkour on the internet. I'm a laughing stock.'

'I think that sort of thing happens a lot, Matt. I can't imagine anybody actually thinks you're a sub-Partridge, damning indictment of the depths to which our democracy has slumped.'

'No?'

'Of course not. You're statuesque.'

He ran his fingers around the collar of his turtleneck and pushed his lank hair into a side parting that immediately fell forward.

'Yes, that's what I thought.'

'I bet whoever did it is some forty-year-old nerd who still lives at home with his mum.'

'Wow, that's a terrific joke, Secret.'

'Here, have a bite of my Subway. It'll calm you down.'

'Thank you, Secret. I forgot my Huel today.'

The door opened and a red-eyed Christian Wakeford walked in. He gasped.

'Matt? Secret?'

Matt couldn't speak because his mouth was full of Christian's sandwich.

'It's not what it looks like, Christian,' I said as a partially munched meatball fell from my mouth.

'Isn't it?'

'OK it is.'

'I see. I see it all now. Us Redwallers, we're just a big joke to the Home Counties crowd aren't we?'

I nodded.

'You're supposed to be handling the investigation into these food thefts, Mr Hancock. Yet you're the one committing them. Which means ...' He stopped and took a deep breath as the full gravity of what he was about to say dawned on him. 'Which means that corruption in the Conservative Party goes right to the very top.'

He turned on his cheap Kickers heel and staggered out in shock. Matt turned to me, still struggling to speak through his mouthful: 'Have you just implicated me in a sandwich scandal?'

'Yes, Matt. But listen. If you keep quiet about this the possibilities are endless. Penny Mordaunt's M&S salads, Nadine's Budgens pasta bakes, Thérèse Coffey's black market black puddings. With you in charge of the investigation into your own behaviour, we could be eating free lunches for the rest of our working lives.'

'A free lunch. They said there was no such thing.'

'And we could be the men who proved them wrong.'

'Yes, we could. Who's them?'

'I've no idea.'

'OK, Secret Tory. But this goes no further than this room.'

'And what about Wakeford?' I asked.

'Leave him to me,' said Matt mysteriously.

Wednesday, 19 January 2022

Quite the most incredible day. We kept hearing that Graham Brady had almost received the requisite number of letters of no confidence in the PM.

Then at PMQs, Christian Wakeford crossed the floor to join Labour. I looked straight at Matt who tried to wink at me, but he can't wink so he just screwed up his face and blinked several times.

Then David Davis stood up and said to Boris, 'You have sat there too long for all the good you have done; in the name of God, go.'

It's all happening so quickly; I don't know which side to put myself on. As an elected representative of the people, my first and last duty is to say or do the thing most likely to save my own skin.

Thursday, 20 January 2022

Went for my elevenses in Portcullis House and found Jodie there with Lisa Nandy and Rachel Reeves.

'Oi. What are you doing here?' I asked, indignant that she hadn't told me she was coming in.

'Hi, Secret, I'm just having a meeting.'

'I can see that. Well, anyway, I'm glad you're here. Someone has blocked my calls to your phone. Whenever I try and ring it I can't get through.'

She looked sheepish, probably not wanting to admit she'd been dating someone so high profile in front of the nobodies she was sitting with.

'Oh, right. I'll look into it. I'll call you, yeah?'

'Great.'

I looked at them for a while and they looked at me, and as nobody was saying anything, I said, 'What?' and then wandered over to the counter to buy a Wagon Wheel, where I could still hear them talking.

'Right, where were we? You are an articulate woman who can connect with people from all walks of life, you speak candidly and passionately not only about the issues that are important to you, but also on things you've only just touched upon. Jodie, on top of all the help you've given us recently …' They laughed and looked at me. 'We'd be very happy to put your name forward to the interview stage.'

I was about to go back over and ask, 'Help with what?' when Stephen Crabb ran in shouting 'Nuggy', put me in a headlock and did a knuckle rub on my scalp.

By the time I'd struggled free, they were gone.

Friday, 21 January 2022

In keeping with the general sense of chaos surrounding the party at the moment, William Wragg has gone on record accusing the whips of bullying and intimidation.

Party elder statesman Nicholas Soames set the record straight by saying that if you think a toxic work environment is an anachronism that compromises effective government, you're weak.

It's raised some very difficult questions. Not least, who is William Wragg?

Saturday, 22 January 2022

Spent all day trying to reach Geoffrey Cox after I got another letter about that parking ticket. I finally got through to him during *Soccer Saturday*. He was speaking from a tennis court on a superyacht.

'Yes, yes, Secret, I'm afraid I've exhausted all the available avenues. There's nothing else I can do.'

'Geoff, I gave you two grand.'

'Well, I might be able to lean on them again for another six.'

'Do you think it'd work?'

'I'd say it's worth a try.'

I don't have a spare six grand at the moment. But then I remembered my sensei Neil Hamilton's second rule of politics: 'Always give off the impression you're loaded even when you're not.'

'Sure. Let's do it.'

I hung up and began to wonder where I was going to get the money from when, apropos of nothing, the phone rang again.

'Hi, Secret Tory, this is Yevgeny Prigozhin. We met at Alisher Usmanov's house.'

'Oh. Hi, Yevgeny.'

'Listen, I've been talking to Mick at Joburg Munitions Executive and if you're keen, I've got a little job for you.'

'What a coincidence. I'm looking for a bit of work. What sort of fee are we talking?'

'How about six thousand pounds?'

'Done.'

Sunday, 23 January 2022

What a day. At 8 a.m. a courier dropped off a brand-new phone at my house which then began receiving instructions.

First up, I had to get in the car and retrieve an aluminium suitcase from a Biffa bin behind the Porton Down Garden and Aquatics Centre in Wiltshire.

Then I was instructed to go and sit on a bench beneath the south door of Salisbury Cathedral, the place that Anastasia had alluded to at the dinner in November. *Why are they so preoccupied with this place?* I wondered as I sat down a bit late after stopping for a Double Decker and a Monster in a Tesco Extra.

The moment my buttocks hit the bench a large man in a tee-shirt with blue and white horizontal stripes, a blue beret and a big beard stood up. Then nothing happened for ages.

Twenty-five minutes later the man came back and pointed at a piece of paper on the seat.

'What's that?'

He pointed again. I looked and saw it was instructions.

'Ohhh, right. I see.' I winked at him. 'It's like *Challenge Anneka*, this. What does it say?'

'Read it,' he said in a thick Russian accent.

'You're here now. Can't you just tell me?'

'No.'

'Go on.'

'No.'

'Please?'

He exhaled loudly. 'It is a note telling you that you need to be taking the briefcase to Stonehenge but because you are late you must be leaving now immediately.'

'Cheers mate. What's your name?'

He looked at my neck, as if assessing its thickness, then picked up the chocolate wrapper I'd dropped on the floor and walked away without a word.

'My name's Secret Tory,' I shouted after him. He didn't hear. I shouted it again, causing several Anglicans to turn their heads, but the sound didn't seem to reach him.

I hopped back in the Overfinch and drove to Stonehenge. The place irritates me. They're always going on about moving the A303 and using public money to 'preserve the historic landscape', but I can't help thinking if it mattered that much they wouldn't have built it so close to the road in the first place.

When I parked up curiosity got the better of me. I couldn't help looking inside the briefcase. It contained some large vials, which I accidently opened upside down and spilled all over the car. I panicked, but then, noticing that the liquid was an almost identical colour to the can of Monster I was drinking, I filled them up with that and hoped they wouldn't notice.

I walked over to the stones and two men with blond buzzcuts doing pull-ups on a lintel jumped down when they saw me. They had 'Wagner Mercenary Group' tee-shirts stretched over their massive pecs, which immediately raised my suspicions that they might be part of the Wagner Mercenary Group. One of them had hands like cannonballs, which I couldn't take my eyes off. They scanned me dispassionately.

'All right, lads, I've had a right faff trying to get in here. I tried to explain to the receptionist that she should let me in for free because I was only here to swap the suitcase with some Russians and I wasn't going to look around, but she was having none of it.'

They looked at each other. I was still transfixed by the fists. The owner raised them and began rolling them around in front of me.

'This is Boris,' said his friend.

'I know a Boris too.'

'Well this is also Boris. He injects his hands with Vaseline. One slap, you sleep.'

'Right, yes. I don't think my Boris does that. Well, here

you go. I'll give the suitcase to you; I doubt Boris can get his hand inside the handle.'

He opened the case and looked at the vials of Pipeline Punch Monster. He seemed satisfied.

'Mother Russia is grateful.'

'Is she? Nice one. I'll be off then. If you fancy it, Danny Kruger tipped me off about a Harvester at the Solstice Business Park. Apparently it's first-class.'

'No, we will be looking around now.'

'Really? It's so boring.'

'We are keen students of the Preseli bluestones and are liking to learn how the Welshmen got them here.'

'Well, it definitely wasn't down the M4 on a bank holiday, I'll tell you that for free. Right then, lads, see you later.'

As I ate my 7 oz gammon steak in the Solstice Business Park and fantasised about having a getaway at the spectacular Holiday Inn there, I texted Prigozhin to tell him the job was done and reflected on my day.

I really like lobbying. It's a great excuse to get out in the fresh air and meet new people.

Monday, 24 January 2022

Got called in to see Boris. He was playing with a mini office basketball set with Brandon Lewis.

'Hi, boss. How can I help?'

'Hello, Secret Tory. It's this. Some of us are quite good friends with the Russians, and all this kerfuffle with Putin building up his troops on the Ukrainian border is causing a bit of the old tensioneroony.'

'Oh yes. I'd forgotten about that. You don't think Putin will do anything, do you?'

He tapped a recent photo of the Cabinet, a handpicked selection of stunningly inconsequential men and women.

'Not if he wants to contend with the full force of the British government in beast mode.'

'He'll be quaking, boss.'

'Now about these Russians.'

'Oh yes. I was doing some lobbying for some of them at Porton Down yesterday as it happens.'

'Ra Ra Rasputin,' sang Boris loudly, as if trying to drown me out.

'I said I did a favour for some of them at Porton Down yesterday.'

He turned to Brandon. 'Are we sure he's the right man for this?'

Brandon stopped blowing bubbles through a straw into his Lucozade and shrugged.

'Whatever the job is, I'm pretty sure I am,' I said, confident of my ability to overpromise in any situation.

'Yes. You are jolly unscrupulous, even for a Tory. Oh, I can't be bothered asking anyone else now. Listen, Secret, it's this. MI5 have compiled a dossier of Tories they think have been compromised by the Russians. It's the sort of piffle the public really don't need to know about but might think they did if they ever found out about it.'

'It's one of those "good idea at the time but in hindsight massive misjudgement" things,' said Brandon.

'Like Brexit?'

'Yes. Or kids,' said Boris. 'Anyway, I've become very good friends with the head of MI5 since we honeytrapped him with Esther McVey, and he has kindly closed down the operation and liberated the files.' He slid one of those data sticks you can get now across the table. 'This is all that is left of their Dissident Dossier. I was wondering if you, as the last Tory anybody ever thinks of, would like to make it disappear for us?'

'Er, yes.'

He gave me that searching look everyone always gives me. 'And would you like to also name a price?'

'Can we get a new vending machine for the corridor?'

'Yes.'

I tried to think what Portillo would say. 'And a new speed camera on the bypass?'

'Yes.'

'And some dogshit bins?'

He let out a laugh and passed me the data stick. 'Yes, Secret, we can.'

'Mum's the word,' I said, tapping my nose with the dossier, which I then dropped on the floor, kicked under a bookcase and spent the next sixty seconds trying to retrieve.

'I won't do that again,' I assured them as I dusted myself down and left.

Tuesday, 25 January 2022

After surveying the disarray the party is in, it is clear to me that Boris is on the ropes. I've come to the only sensible conclusion. Using the Dissident Dossier to blackmail my colleagues, I'm going to launch my own leadership bid.

I think it's best not to plan these things five years in advance like Liz and Rishi, and instead go into your challenge with no strategy whatsoever.

I spent the morning racking my brain to work out who would be my ideal campaign manager. It needs to be someone who exudes political nous, someone who can think on their feet, someone who won't walk straight into any media traps. There was only one option. I got straight on the phone to Lee Anderson.

Wednesday, 26 January 2022

I found the MP for Ashfield in Brent Cross Shopping Centre – his second home is in Neasden because he's drawn to London's cultural hubs – and waited for him to finish gossiping with the staff at JD Sports, where he is a regular.

His energy and enthusiasm are like nothing I've ever seen in politics before. The extent of his learning is formidable, from statues to telling poor people how to cook food they don't have, and from taking the knee to the national anthem – he's across the detail on everything.

He thinks I should stand on a culture war ticket, and I think he's right. I'm absolutely buzzing to have someone like him in my corner.

Thursday, 27 January 2022

'Are you fucking kidding?' snapped Portillo after I announced I was thinking of running for leader. 'You can't even handle your own backlogged constituency business and you're coming in here with some half-baked idea about running for Prime Minister?'

'If this is about the driving ban, there was nothing I could do about it.'

'No, it's not about that. Well, yes, it is, but that's not the point.'

'Listen, son, this is above your pay grade, you wouldn't understand.'

'Dad, Deliveroo is above my pay grade. So don't patronise me. The only reason this constituency isn't rioting is because of Everton, and you don't even pay him.'

'Hello, Mr Tory,' said Everton cheerfully from behind a mountain of my paperwork.

'Everton likes it here. He gets a roof over his head and free water. He'll never find another boss like me.'

'You're a piece of work, you know that?'

'Listen, I've got Lee Anderson as my campaign manager and Andrew Rosindell says he'll think about supporting my bid if I promise to back the enforced repatriation of all post-World War II immigrants. It's in the bag.'

'Dad, we've been running this place without you for a month. You haven't been in since Christmas. The roof still isn't fixed, Lucy's hip is unbearable in the cold, Everton has been doing sixty-hour weeks, you've stopped answering your phone and you never look at your emails.'

'You got that template I sent, didn't you?'

'Yes.'

'Well, there you go. And I've got a new speed camera for the bypass. Though you ought to be careful with that when you get your licence back. Now listen: I need you to make me a copy of this.'

I handed him the data stick thing.

'What is it?'

'Nothing important. Make a copy and I'll get the roof fixed,' I lied.

'Right. Well, as you know, we've only got an IBM 386 so I'll have to copy it onto floppies.'

'Argh, stop boring me with detail and get on with it.'

After a lot of tutting to speed him up, he presented me with a little box of 3.5-inch disks upon which I wrote

Command & Conquer to misdirect the undercover operatives I presume are constantly tailing me.

Friday, 28 January 2022

On my way to James Cleverly's office for our irregular UNO-versity of Life card school I noticed the Department for Work and Pensions store cupboard door was ajar.

That's odd, I thought. *Thérèse is very thrifty, she usually keeps this place under lock and key.*

I put my ear to the door. I could hear an enthused voice saying, 'Do you like my mutant algorithm?'

'Oh yes sire. Joust me, joust me.'

I moved to investigate further but put too much weight on the door and fell through it.

In a working life that started in illegal live animal exports and included six years as Ann Widdecombe's aide, I thought I'd seen it all. But finding Thérèse Coffey sitting on a box of unexamined Universal Credit disability assessments with her arms draped around Gavin Williamson's neck was certainly a new one on me.

We all spoke at once.

'We're just looking at some work capability evaluations,' said Thérèse.

'I'm looking for some laminator paper,' said Gavin.

'I was the voice that said "Vorsprung durch Technik" in those Audi adverts,' I said.

There was a long, awkward pause, during which Gavin was still lightly gyrating his hips.

'So, do you want to leave us to it?' asked Thérèse.

'Er, yes, certainly.' But in my haste to depart, I inadvertently pushed the door shut and needed to enter the keycode to get out. I hammered it several times, but it didn't work, largely because I was in shock and hitting numbers at random.

'Two-three-six-eight-zero,' said Thérèse impatiently.

'Sorry, bye,' I said as I jabbed it in and made for the relative sanity of the Westminster corridor.

The whole thing was so embarrassing. Possibly worse than the time I caught Neil Parish wanking over tractors.

Saturday, 29 January 2022

Mike Fabricant texted to say that I'm 500/1 to be the next PM. Better than that, when I went to check my online banking to see how much I could afford to lump on, I found that six grand had been deposited by Joburg Munitions Advisers. As I was transferring it to Coxy for the parking ticket, I thought about putting it on the Register of Members' Interests and decided not to.

Sunday, 30 January 2022

Feeling like I ought to do at least a little bit of work on my leadership bid, I went into the constituency office when the others weren't in.

But after noticing that the spray can of whoever is doing the *SCUM*s is running out, stepping over the broken glass from the weekend's smashed windows, and opening a couple of letters – from some primary school children asking me to stop pollution and that interminable man whose wife is languishing in an Iranian prison – I got bored, and decided to hone my leadership skills by playing *Command & Conquer*.

I know I've said this before, but I really am an excellent general and I'd be very surprised if something doesn't come of this leadership bid.

Monday, 31 January 2022

Hotdesking in Wetherspoons this afternoon when Gavin sat next to me, ordered a Fruit Shoot, opened his laptop and began searching for static holiday homes on the Cleveland coastline.

'What are you doing, just writing a letter of no confidence to Graham Brady?' he said suddenly.

'Yeah,' I lied, closing *Command & Conquer*. 'You?'

'Same,' he lied. 'Listen, Secret, about the other day.'

'Yes.'

'It's Thérèse.'

'Go on.'

'I love her.'

I held his hand. 'Gavin. I know. And I can see why. But you're a father. You've got a family to think about.'

'I know, I know.'

'Didn't you have an affair before, when you were working at that fireplace company?'

'Yes. But that was nothing compared to this. When I'm with Thérèse, the whole world just feels new. Her compassion, her sensitivity, her wit, her empathy. When we're together, I just feel whole.'

'I had exactly the same thing with Liz Truss, Gavin. But then I met someone else and didn't any more. I'm afraid you're going to have to ask yourself some very difficult questions though.'

'Science and Nature?'

'No.'

'Sport? Not Art and Lit?'

'No Gav. About Thérèse. Is it just a flash in the pan, or are you willing to destroy the lives of everyone close to you to pursue love with a woman incapable of summoning a scintilla of sympathy for Mercy Baguma?'

'Oh, not that, Secret. Thérèse was having a terrible day, she was getting badgered to introduce functioning sanitation in her buy-to-lets and then she got ambushed with an impossible question about whether she felt compassion for a destitute woman who died alone with her infant child in her arms because the British state had abandoned her.'

'I know, Gav. I'm just playing devil's advocate. Thérèse is a catch, we all know that. But listen son, you're a Tory so you know what you've got to do: whatever you want, and then lie about it as much as possible.'

'Thank you, Secret. I knew I could rely on you for some perspective.'

'And obviously I'll try to leverage you with it at some point.'

'Of course.'

I woke my computer up.

'Is that *Command & Conquer: Red Alert*?'

'Guilty.'

'I used to love that. Could I borrow it?'

'Of course,' I said, digging out the box of installation disks from my briefcase. 'Good luck with whatever you decide. I don't care what they say, you're one of the good guys.'

'OK, bye … Hang on a minute, what do they say?'

'That you're an overpromoted human trainwreck.'

'Oh, good. That's not as bad as I thought.'

February 2022

Tuesday, 1 February 2022

Boris said in the chamber that Keir Starmer was a complete failure because he turned a blind eye to Jimmy Savile while he was at the CPS, and it's exactly the sort of politics that helps neither the bereaved relatives of Covid nor the forgotten victims of sexual abuse that I am here for.

Wednesday, 2 February 2022

Ran into The Saj practising his power stances in front of the mirror in the Westminster Hall gents before Health Questions.

'Mind if I drop in, The Saj?'

'Not at all, Secret.'

For a few moments we stood side by side, practising placing our feet at improbably wide angles and throwing sultry looks into the mirror. I thought I was doing OK until he had to stop to correct me.

'No, no, no Secret Tory, you're doing it all wrong. Your width is OK but your angles are all over the place. If you just work on a 180-degree plane it looks ridiculous. You need to think about your audience and take different positions all the time. For instance, you might go into a meeting with American private healthcare provider Cigna at 130 degrees, but you'd never talk to the CBI that narrow.'

'The Saj, this is fascinating. I never realised there was so much to it.'

'I know, right? I actually wrote my MBA on it.'

'Really?'

'Yes, I could get you a copy if you like?' He suggested this in that tentative, hopeful way in which somebody who has no friends suggests doing something for you.

'That would be great,' I replied, offering him a bit of my Peperami.

'Wow, what's this?'

'The English Wagyu beef.'

He took a tentative bite. His face lit up. 'Wow. It really is. Secret, I'm organising the Black and White ball next week. Are you coming?'

'Am I?' I asked rhetorically.

'I don't know. Are you?'

'No, I never get invited.'

'Well, I can put you down if you like. Pop up to my office next week and I'll give you a ticket. I could show you that dissertation too.'

'Nice one, The Saj,' I said, lobbing the last bit of Peperami into my mouth.

'Great stuff, see you later …' There was a pause. 'Mate.'

'Yep, bye then colleague,' I replied, not wanting to encourage him.

Thursday, 3 February 2022

Nadine rang. She's furious about my leadership bid. I asked her how she knew and she said she'd found Lee in the Jubilee Cafe with some felt tips, asking people how to spell 'leadership' and 'bid'.

I told her that Lee was confused.

'After everything Boris has done for people like us, Secret, he focking better be. You don't want to know what I'm capable of.'

She was right, I don't. Then in the background, I thought I could hear a voice saying, 'Here comes Dionysus looking for his naughty MaeNad.'

'Who's that, Nads? His voice sounds familiar.'

'No one. I've got to go. Has Alexander been a good boy for his Culture Secretary …?'

Friday, 4 February 2022

Got a call from a very distressed Carrie asking if I'd seen Boris, as someone has put Dilyn the dog in their microwave and she thinks it might have been Nadine.

On an unrelated note, I've decided to end my leadership bid.

Saturday, 5 February 2022

Charlie Stayt interviewed Nadine in her bookless library and asked when she last spoke to the Prime Minister. She got very cagey.

'Why? Why are you asking me that question?'

'I'd like to know.'

'We've communicated.'

'I'm really confused. Is that a difficult question? I'm just asking if you've spoken to the Prime Minister in the last 24 hours.'

'I'm not going to tell you the extent of my communications with the Prime Minister. I mean, I've answered your question. We have communicated. What is your next question?'

It was a formidable performance; I just hope the fifty-inch Flintstones boxers dangling on the bookcase behind her didn't detract from it.

Sunday, 6 February 2022

'Woke psychodrama is a form of Maoism that threatens Western values.' So sayeth Olly Dowden to a climate-science-denying think tank in Washington.

I'd bloody love to work on a nihilistic dark-money-funded lobby group one day, but with his blood-and-thunder opinions to order, Olly has got there before me. Putin's T-15s better not be flying rainbow flags when they roll into Kyiv or they aren't going to know what hits them.

Monday, 7 February 2022

A mob of anti-vaxxers have attacked Keir Starmer and David Lammy. They were screaming things like, 'What's it like working for the New World Order?', 'Jimmy Savile paedo protector!' and, 'We're going to hang you!'

A lot of people were saying Boris should shoulder some of the blame for emboldening this pond life, but that's not fair. The point at which we're not allowed to amplify baseless right-wing conspiracy theories for short-term political gain is the moment when we should all just pack up and go home.

Tuesday, 8 February 2022

Boris's advisers have all quit, but he's taken ownership of the situation by saying it's strong leadership to have all your staff resign.

He's appointed Guto Harri as his new comms adviser, whose game plan is to play to Boris's only strength: banter.

Guto got the ball rolling by doing an interview with Welsh-language site Golwg360, which nobody could understand because speaking more than one language is bad for you. But I cut and pasted it into Google Translate to try to make sense of the PM's new direction and it read as follows:

I walked in, gave him a salute and said, 'Prime Minister, Guto Harri reporting for duty,' and he stood up trouserless from behind a fußball table and said, 'The Archbishop of Banterbury, as I live and breathe.' And I asked, 'Are you going to survive Boris?' and he said, 'Well there's a hole in my soul the size of the track and trace budget but I'll bloody well try!' Then he patted a passing intern on the arse and began singing 'Girls, Girls, Girls' by Mötley Crüe and I joined in.

Harri went on: 'He's not a complete clown. Ninety per cent of our discussion was serious, about saving his career at the expense of our living standards, but he's a character too and there's fun to be had if you ignore the fact he loathes you. When you think about it, all he's ever offered is false bonhomie and sub-Twickers car-park Six Nations banter, so I've gone in there saying let's play to your only strength and see if you can clown your way out of the fact you're a self-pitying narcissist who's been found out. It's a bold gambit, but he's a wannabe Pericles desperate not to be remembered as the Neil Morrissey of PMs, so he's got no choice.

Wednesday, 9 February 2022

Guto has made Boris do a mini-reshuffle. Mark Spencer has been promoted to Leader of the House of Commons while he investigates him over Islamophobia. Chris Heaton-Harris is the new Chief Whip. Jacob Rees-Mogg has been made Minister for Brexit Opportunities (*sic*).

Thursday, 10 February 2022

Went to the Department of Health to see The Saj. The whole place has had a massive makeover since Matt Hancock's time. Gone are the *Trainspotting*, *Top Gun* and monochrome-topless-hunk-holding-a-baby posters, and literally everything has been painted gold.

'What do you think, Secret? Be honest, nuts out of the hot tub, too much?'

'It's perfect, The Saj,' I said, squinting to cope with the gilded glare as I put a Peperami on his desk.

'For me?'

'Sure.'

He adopted an unconventional 92-degree power stance. 'Secret, I'm humbled. No parliamentary colleague has ever been nice to me before.'

He opened a sliding gold cabinet filled with hundreds of identical red leather books with *POWER STANCING – AN MBA BY THE SAJ* written on them in gold 32pt embossed letters. He passed me one.

'Thanks,' I said, knowing I'd definitely never read it.

'Not a problem, not a problem at all, Secret.' He looked around his desk.

'Would you like some Cigna catheter bags too? They're American.'

'That's, er, very kind of you.'

'Well, that's what mates do, isn't it? Give each other presents. And we're mates now, aren't we?'

'Hmm.'

'So, you know I'm organising the auction for the Black and White ball. I was wondering Secret, would you like to donate a prize?'

I had to sit down. There is no greater honour for a Tory than selling their integrity to the highest-bidding Russian at our annual novelty auction.

'Yes, The Saj. With every fibre of my being. Thank you …'

The Saj looked at me hopefully.

'… Workmate.'

Friday, 11 February 2022

Nadine has been sent to Saudi Arabia. Guto says it's so Boris can get a bit of space, although Mike Fabricant says it's because she put Dilyn in a 750w microwave last week. I sent her a WhatsApp saying we'd miss her at the ball and asking if she could check in with Imran to see how he's getting on with the Heckler & Kochs I sold him.

Saturday, 12 February 2022

The big day, the Black and White ball at the V&A, the annual rattle of the fundraising tin, selling fifteen-grand seats and illegal access to ministers under the guise of frivolous auction prizes.

It was the usual cross-section – sociopathic car-insurance magnates, fertiliser czars, Saudi misogynists, Russian crooks – and there were plenty of familiar faces, particularly if you were one of those MPs who toplessly ferried hors d'oeuvres for oligarchs back in November.

Those of us who had been there tried to maintain our dignity, which was a struggle with Alisher Usmanov barking like a dog at Simon Clarke, Roman Abramovich pinching

Brandon Lewis's arse and Dmitri Lebedev instructing Daniel Kerchingski to 'clean under my fingernails next time'.

For some reason there had been a mistake with the seating plan, and in the furthest corner of the room, away from the rows of tables lined with silver cutlery and ice sculptures of St Basil, Andrew Bridgen, James Cleverly, Mark Francois and I sat at a little plastic table with a plastic Spiderman tablecloth.

Anastasia Volkov sought me out after the starters. Carrie tried to steer her away, but Anastasia called her a 'Crayola De Ville' and strode straight past. I'd never heard anyone speak to Princess Nut Nuts like that before.

I hate the food you get at these things, so I'd brought my own Dunkers Jumbo Tubes (not the annoying breadstick ones). I offered Anastasia one. She declined.

'Go on Anastasia, live a little,' said Mark Francois.

'I do not want to hear from this man.'

I turned to Andrew Bridgen and said, 'Andy, give Mark the Game Boy.'

'But I've almost got six lines on *Tetris*.'

'Queen and Kremlin, Andy.'

'Fine,' he harrumphed, reluctantly handing Mark the table Game Boy.

Anastasia watched the engine room of the Tory Party intently as we set the world to rights over 8-bit *Zelda* and *Duck Tales*. I dusted off my best small talk.

'So, L-Bomb, what's Putin like? He gets a lot of bad press, but it seems to me like he's got a can-do attitude. I know Nigel loves him.'

'Yes, he and Nigel are very close. He is a very can-do. I remember when our pool cleaner was late for his shift two weeks in a row, my husband told Putes of this, and let's just say that man was never late for a shift again.'

'Got him to pull his socks up with a firm talking to, did he?'

'He would have, if they weren't covered in concrete.'

'Concrete socks? Does he know Mike Graham?'

'The brightness had left his eyes,' said Anastasia mysteriously. I didn't have a clue what she was on about.

'Are you sure I can't offer you a Jumbo Tube?'

'No. Thank you. Listen, Secret, the Russian state is really very grateful for your help with the moving of this briefcase out of Porton Down.'

'Don't mention it. It was a nice day out, actually.'

'I'm glad. I was wondering, how would you like a donation to your constituency office to fix the roof?'

'How do you know about that?'

'Oh, you know, delinquenting teenagers, FSB agents. These people talk.'

I thought about the rain driving straight through the crumbling Thermatex onto the team and imagined how much better my office would look with a new De'Longhi coffee machine.

'I'm all ears, Anastasia.'

'I'm told you might have a copy of something called a Dissident Dossier.'

'Well, I can neither confirm nor d—'

'Do you or not?'

'Yes.'

'Well, if you could let Mother Russia have a copy of it, we would be very grateful.'

'Yeah, fine,' I said.

'You are a good man, Secret Tory.'

'I know,' I said with an air of vindication.

'Shhhh! It's the auction prizes,' said James Cleverly.

The Saj strode on stage to a chorus of light-hearted boos that lasted five minutes, power stanced at a maverick 150 degrees, and began reading out the reserves:

'Borscht in a Porsche with Liz Truss – £30,000 …

'MDMA sampling with Michael Gove – £20,000 …

'Dogfighting with John Redwood – £10,000 …

'Paintball in Epping Forest with Mark Francois's Apocalypse Delta Force, two-time runners-up in the Essex Masters paintball league – £30 …

'Home makeover with Boris Johnson and Lulu Lytle – £50,000 …

'Frank Spencer theme night with Gavin Williamson – £30,000 …

'A *Come Dine with Me*-style dinner party with Secret Tory – no reserve.'

Sunday, 13 February 2022

Spent the day shitting blood in the Aitken Suite. I thought it might have been the vodka and line of bash I did in the toilets with Evgeny Lebedev, but then I got a WhatsApp from Steve Barclay saying his 'chodbin was fucking crimson after all that borscht LOL'.

A blessed relief.

Monday, 14 February 2022

Gave Elsie and Lucy their Valentine's gifts of a new catheter bag each.

'I don't use one of these,' said Elsie.

'Neither do I,' said Lucy.

'Fine,' I said, displeased by their lack of gratitude. 'Blow them up and use them as pillows.'

'Another day, another distressed constituent with raw sewage backing up into their council flat,' said Portillo as he breezed in and hung up the local radio baseball cap that makes him look seriously ill on my Abu Hamza coat hooks.

'Dad? What are you doing here?'

'Never mind that. What time do you call this?' I said, tapping my watch. 'You need to buck your ideas up my boy. OK, guys, listen in. We're going to be getting quite a considerable donation to the office from some Russians.'

'Does that mean we can fix the roof, Mr Tory?' asked Elsie.

'Could we pay Everton?' asked Lucy.

'What about some new computers?' asked Portillo.

I gave it to them straight. 'I'm afraid there probably won't be enough money left if I decide to get the diamond-encrusted Bluetooth headset I've been looking at, but I promise you that if there is, I'll think about it.'

Tuesday, 15 February 2022

Sadiq Khan has forced Cressida Dick out of the Met, simply because she's presided over a culture of misogyny, racism, homophobia and harassment. It's PC gone mad.

Wednesday, 16 February 2022

Got a message on the phone Prigozhin's courier dropped off last month, telling me to take the Dissident Dossier to my lunch spot.

I rocked up at the Bomber Command Memorial at noon and watched Johnny Mercer doing his drills. Today he was performing burpees while calling out the names of his favourite Rugby Union players.

'Carling, Dallaglio, Underwood …'

I felt a sharp, hard barrel in the small of my back. 'Mr Tory, I am here for the report.'

'Robinson, Leonard, Ubogu …'

I turned round and realised I was leaning on an anti-homeless spike. To my left was a young woman with a shock of dyed blonde hair and black eyebrows drinking a Pepsi Max.

'Guscott, Itoje, the other Underwood …'

'Hi, are you one of Yevgeny and Anastasia's friends?' I said.

'I am here for the report.'

I gave her the box of floppy disks from my briefcase. 'I'll take that as a yes.'

'Mother Russia for this report will be very grateful comrade.'

'Matt Dawson,' yelled an exhausted Mercer as he collapsed into an exhausted heap after a furious final burst of effort.

Thursday, 17 February 2022

The Brexit bonuses keep coming. We've just ended the spiteful EU regulation banning the sale of foie gras. The Redwall have been crying out for geese who've had food mechanically pumped through metal pipes into their gullets until their livers have swollen to bursting point, and we've given it to them.

Friday, 18 February 2022

Cressida's leaving drinks were a low-key affair, just the ninety of us in the Cabinet Room. It was lovely, reminiscent of those balmy days at the height of lockdown. Liz Truss was there, and at one point our hands brushed each other's as we reached for sausage rolls.

Saturday, 19 February 2022

I think I might be moving on from Jodie. I've started having dreams about Liz again.

Last night she was paragliding over a thirty-mile tailback on the M20 on a Union Jack parachute like Roger Moore at the start of *The Spy Who Loved Me*, but she was wearing a bottle-green siren suit rather than a mustard-yellow camel jacket.

In other news, Prince Andrew has just paid £12 million to a woman he has never met other than in photos.

Sunday, 20 February 2022

Covid is over. All restrictions are to end, including the requirement to isolate. It goes against the best advice of all his scientific advisers, but Boris follows his hunches and, personally, I'd prefer to follow the guidance of a man who insisted on shaking everyone's hands at the height of a pandemic than the sort of dweebs in lab coats who watch *Only Connect*.

Monday, 21 February 2022

Tensions have ratcheted up on the Ukrainian border. Over a hundred thousand Russian troops have now amassed there. But Putin be warned: when you come at Liz Truss, you better not miss. She's talking a very tough game in her plangent new Mrs Thatcher voice, and I honestly don't think he has the slightest idea what he's up against.

Tuesday, 22 February 2022

Putin is insane. He's gone up against Liz Truss and moved his troops into eastern Ukraine.

We've responded with shock and awe by sanctioning three oligarchs and a handful of Russian banks nobody has heard of. As of 7 p.m., none of the sanctioned banks was Arron. Although, as Matt Hancock pointed out over a stolen packet of Turkey Twizzlers we shared in the disabled loo at lunchtime, considering the sanctions we imposed on ourselves with Brexit, it's surprising we didn't feel confident enough to go further.

Wednesday, 23 February 2022

It is all-out war in Ukraine. Here's what we know so far:

Putin has committed tens of thousands of men into
Ukraine through Belarus, Russia and the Crimea.
Liz Truss has committed tens of thousands of pounds to
photoshoots in *OK!, Hello!* and Conservative Home.
I have committed my twenty-grand Dodgy Dossier fee to
a taxidermied polar-bear-skin rug from Canada.

Thursday, 24 February 2022

The images of terror, panic and death coming from Ukraine are ghastly. Which is weird because in all the films I watch, war looks fun.

It is early days, but social media is full of images of stranded Russian tanks getting towed by Ukrainian tractors, and it's beginning to look like Putin has failed to provide his conscripts with enough fuel, food or tactics. As Ben Wallace said over a Moscow mule with Dom Raab at lunch, 'That's the sort of thing we'd do.'

I confided in the lads about the twenty grand I'd just got from Prigozhin, and Dom said he'd once got twenty-five off a crook called Leus who spent four years in prison for laundering money from Turkmenistan.

'Do you think you'll ever have to pay it back?'

'No. I spent it on a five-star holiday to Crete. The only possible way I could afford to pay it back would be by selling the Maserati. And that's a red line I'm not willing to cross.'

Friday, 25 February 2022

Jacob Rees-Mogg has given everyone some much-needed perspective on this continental land war in Europe by announcing that he is looking into the repeal of decimalisation. At long last we can stop working in the incomprehensible European metric system of tens and return to the common-sense realm of pecks, bushels, perches and quarts.

Saturday, 26 February 2022

The world is being inspired by Ukrainian president Volodymyr Zelensky. He is staying in Kyiv to fight. He keeps walking around recording videos of himself to rally his people, and that is despite the city being full of Russian mercenaries sent there to kill him. Everyone is captivated by his courage, and I think it highlights the cultural differences between us and the Ukrainians. When we're under curfew, our leaders just get hammered.

On an unrelated note, in one of the videos I thought I saw that bloke I met on a bench at Salisbury Cathedral last month! What are the chances?

Sunday, 27 February 2022

I saw Mrs Burke while I was pouring the fat from my deep-fat fryer over our hedge this afternoon.

'Afternoon,' I said cagily, wondering if she could see what I was doing to her daffodils.

'Oh, Secret, I've just been watching the news. It's ghastly. You'd have thought a country willing to become an international pariah by behaving entirely out of self-interest and damning its neighbours to hell would at least have had a long-term plan.'

'Please, can we stop talking about Brexit, Mrs Burke? It's every time I see you. We won, get over it.'

'I'm talking about Russia.'

'Oh that. Yes, it's not great.'

'I keep reading that the government is up to its neck in Russian favours. Have you ever seen anything?'

'Never.'

My phone rang.

'Sorry, I've got to take this. Yes, the polar bear rug. Yes, well I came into an unexpected bit of cash, and I've always wanted one. It's been shipped already? Thank you so much, I'll keep an eye out.'

Monday, 28 February 2022

The Russians have been launching cluster bombs and thermobaric weapons at Kharkiv and Mariupol. Worse than that, despite the EU's appalling record on being nice to refugees, the Ukrainians have hatched an insane plan to join it.

Nigel is livid. He wants to know why you'd choose to surrender your nation's sovereignty to the EU rather than malign Russian interests.

March 2022

Tuesday, 1 March 2022

Lucy's hip is getting worse and she still hasn't got a date for the operation. Watching Elsie walk her into work, operating her own Zimmer one-handed so that she can give Lucy an extra one with hers, I thought they made quite the pair.

Everton and Portillo rushed out into the rain to assist them, but I had to call them back because DPD had just arrived with my rug and I needed their help to get it in.

I walked around on it barefoot all morning, imagining I was the brave hunter who downed it with nothing but a team of thirty locals and a high-velocity rifle.

Wednesday, 2 March 2022

Say what you like about war – thousands dying, millions of people displaced, entire communities destroyed – it's great for bringing people together. There isn't really anything to disagree about on Putin. One minute you're slagging him off to the woman stacking shelves in Londis, the next you're passing her thoughts off as your own to the man on the checkout in Texaco. After six years of division, it's a welcome source of unity. What a shame it's taken an avoidable hell on earth for the people of Ukraine to get us here.

Thursday, 3 March 2022

Gavin Williamson has been knighted. Everyone confused.

Friday, 4 March 2022

Gavin surprised me in my office while I was pretending to hunt my polar bear.

'Gavin, this is a surprise,' I said, standing up from the carpet.

'Sir Gavin.'

'Sir Gavin. Yes, congratulations on that. What was it for, messing up those exams?'

'Let's say ...' He paused. 'I've levelled up.'

'Of course. How's the battle going with the Russians for control of the European mainland?'

'What?'

'*Command & Conquer*, I lent you the disks.'

'Yes, that's why I'm here. I've brought them back.' He simpered for some reason, but I ignored him because he's annoying like that.

'Who were you playing as, Allies or Russians?'

'You could say I was playing them off against each other.'

'Yeah. The Russian units are more durable and powerful aren't they? But they're also slower-moving and more expensive.'

I looked at the disks in my hand and did a double take. 'Hang on. This is the Dissident Dossier.'

'Yes, it is. Thanks for the knighthood, Secret. There's some juicy information in them thar files. It turns out it's quite easy to leverage a knighthood out of Boris if you know about the Cowabungabunga party at Evgeny's place, so thanks to you, I am now Sir Gavin Williamson of Filey: licence to crenellate.'

'Shit,' I said, as I realised that not only had I given the dossier to Sir Gavin, but I must have given a copy of *Command & Conquer* to the Russians.

'Does Boris know I was the one who gave it to you?' I asked, as it also dawned on me that I could have asked for more than a speed camera, two dogshit bins and a vending machine.

'Not yet. What's it worth to keep quiet?'

'Piss off, Gavin.'

'Sir Gavin.'

'You won't tell him.'

'Why not?'

'Because I know about you and Thérèse. I'm sure the tabloids would love to hear about Sir Williamson of Filey's infidelities in the very week he got knighted.'

'No, Secret – please, no. I just need more time to tell Joanne and the girls.'

'Well then. We've got an understanding. As we teeter on the edge of World War III, you keep quiet about me compromising our government's sordid secrets, and I'll keep quiet about you and Thérèse.'

Saturday, 5 March 2022

Went on a frack-finding mission to Lancashire with Richard Tice.

Dick's farsighted belief that a healthy bank account is more important than a healthy planet has uncharacteristically led him to use the unfolding tragedy in Ukraine to further his campaign to end our net zero commitments.

To achieve this he wants to increase our dependence on fossil fuels – and what better time to do that than in the middle of a war with an enemy who is the world's biggest exporter of them?

He says political will is vital, since there's only enough fracking treasure in the Lancashire hills to supply the country for a year. Once we've plundered Barnoldswick we'll have to look elsewhere, and he's asking for my support.

I was unsure at first. I don't usually have an opinion on things until I've spoken to a whip, but then he offered me a lift home from Colne in his helicopter and I said yes.

The moment we were airborne I sent Mark Francois a selfie pretending I was on spec-ops in Ukraine. But he didn't believe me. He said he could see the Reebok Stadium out of the window, and that's in Bolton.

Sunday, 6 March 2022

Sarah Vine has written in the *Mail on Sunday* about how the RSPCA has gone woke. Apparently, they came to her house and seized two Labrador puppies because they weren't wearing LGBTQ+ rainbow harnesses.

It's disgusting how far these social-justice warriors have infiltrated our flagship institutions. As with the scandals at the National Trust, RNLI and NSPCC, if I'd had membership of any of them, I'd have cancelled it there and then.

Monday, 7 March 2022

Thank goodness for Conservatives. Never mind lockdown parties, lobbying and billions on track and trace; at last we've got round to doing what we're good at: exporting arms. Boris is sending NLAWs and Javelins to bolster Ukraine's war effort.

Even better than that, out of 1.5 million displaced Ukrainians, we've taken 50. Priti and the Home Office are understandably worried about how many drug dealers and Russian agents might be among them, and Daniel Kerchingski made the excellent point that it would be dishonest to accept Ukrainians when there are so many countries between here and there, because once the war is over it would take them longer to get home.

You really can't beat that cuddly feeling you get from turning back a family who've crossed a continent with only the clothes on their backs.

Tuesday, 8 March 2022

There's been a bit of pushback on our refugee effort. Which, considering we've spent the last decade courting xenophobic votes, has surprised us all. The Ukrainians are tugging on the nation's heart strings in a way that Syrians and Yemenis don't. I've no idea why.

Yvette Cooper asked if we'd set up anything in Calais yet and Priti said we had a temporary processing centre, although it later transpired that this was an unmanned desk with some Kit Kats on it.

Chris Bryant said that this was a national disgrace and that the Home Office, Potemkin-like, were lining the road with fake reception centres.

MP for Gainsborough and super-empath Sir Edward Leigh returned fire. He said he had no idea who Potemkin was, but as far as he was concerned he could fuck off because Lincolnshire was full.

Wednesday, 9 March 2022

Olly has asked me to join Daniel Kerchingski's Oligarch Sanction Taskforce. He assured me that it wasn't a stunt to distract from how few Russians we've sanctioned so far, but in fact a group of highly trained Tory operatives tackling oligarchs without fear or favour whenever and wherever we encounter them. I asked Olly if that meant we were sanctioning them or helping them avoid sanctions. He replied, 'A bit of both really, Secret.'

Thursday, 10 March 2022

I've passed basic training and am now a fully fledged member of the OST.

The course was quite straightforward. Ben Elliot taught us several deferential ways of addressing ultra-wealthy men in Russian. Then we spent the afternoon at Roman Abramovich's Kensington mansion loading Gola holdalls into a Transit van, after which we drove them down to the river and reloaded them onto a speedboat.

I was doing it with Daniel and a driver from the Home Office who was supposed to be building a reception centre in Calais, but Priti had redirected him here.

At one point a wad of fifties fell out of one of the black and orange holdalls.

'Great Scotland, I've no idea how they got in there,' said Roman. 'I must have got them out to donate to Amnesty International. Honestly, I'd forget my own head if it wasn't nailed on. Here you go blokes, have one of these for your troubles.' And he handed us a £2 coin each while carefully pocketing the large wad of notes.

'Thank you so much, Sire,' said Daniel, who performed a bow so deep that when he stood up, he had the filth from a blocked drain impartially smeared across his forehead.

All in, it was an excellent day. And to top it off, when the captain of the boat arrived, it was none other than John Terry. Let's just say it would have been rude not to get selfies.

Friday, 11 March 2022

I was at the Bomber Command Memorial eating my lunch when I saw on my phone that the Russians had destroyed a Ukrainian maternity hospital. An abhorrent act. I thought about all the hospitals we must have destroyed while bombing German cities in 1943 and 1944, and how the monument that was in front of me commemorated, or lionised (depending on how early each year you put your poppy on), the young men told to do it. Two different wars, decades apart, fighting for different reasons. But what difference would that have made when the bombs went off? What had any of those victims done?

It was a lot of thoughts all at once, none of which I was particularly comfortable with, so I scrolled my phone and saw a headline saying that Roman Abramovich had just been sanctioned. Apparently, he's got a 'father and son' relationship with Putin, but nobody knew about it until this morning. What a shame; he was so nice to me yesterday.

I hope he had some warning to sneak a little bit of his money out of the UK. He's earned it.

Saturday, 12 March 2022

Got a message from Portillo asking if I fancied a pint, but with *The Rock* on Sky Classics again, I ignored it.

Sunday, 13 March 2022

Portillo came over this afternoon.

'You forgot, didn't you?'

'No.'

'Dad, don't lie. It's obvious you did. It's fine.'

'No, I didn't forget. Forget what?'

'My birthday.'

'Oh, right, yes. No, I didn't forget.'

'Dad, I saw *The Rock* was on. How many times have you seen it now? Forty?'

'No. Is that how old you are?'

'Dad, I'm twenty-three.'

'Is that all? Are you sure? It feels like longer.'

'Thanks.'

'Don't sulk. If I'd forgotten, how on earth would I have known to get you this mobile phone?' I said, handing him the mobile the Russians gave me to do my lobbying on.

'A Nokia 3310.'

'Don't be like that. I went to a lot of effort to get you it.'

'OK, thanks. Have you got a charger for it?'

'No.'

Monday, 14 March 2022

Gavin Williamson collared me on my way to my daily dressing-down from Chris Heaton-Harris. He looked worried.

'What is it, Gavin?'

'Sir Gavin.'

'Sir Gavin.'

'It's Thérèse. She thinks she might be pregnant.'

'What?'

He nodded gravely.

'Seriously?'

'She's asked me to get her a pregnancy test, but I don't want to risk getting caught buying one. It wouldn't look good. Secret, you're single, do you think you could do it for me?'

'Yeah, I guess so. You'll owe me.'

'Yes, yes.'

'OK, come with me.'

We walked up to the Star Pharmacy near St James's Park, and Mr Kyriacou put my regular 55-ml pipe of Germoloids on the counter.

'Not today, Costas, I'm pretty tight at the moment. Have you got any pregnancy tests?'

'Aha, you been going on that Tinder, Secret?'

'Something like that,' I said, secretly thrilled my chemist might think I am sexually active.

'They're between the fortified iron and the Tampax.'

'Mr Kyriacou, please don't be so coarse. Nobody wants to hear feminine hygiene products being referred to by their brand names.'

'Sorry, Mr Tory. Please – have some free lateral flow tests.'

I grabbed a handful from the cardboard box on the counter and put them in the pocket of my Barbour, along with the pregnancy test.

'Here you go, Sir Gavin,' I said when I stepped outside, reaching into my pocket to pass him the Clearblue.

'No, no, no,' he hissed as Tim Farron walked past, his head buried in a Bible. 'Discreetly.'

'Fine. Put your hand in my pocket. It's in there.'

Sir Gavin dipped his hand into my pocket while I did the there's-nothing-to-see-here whistle.

'Thank you, Secret.'

'No problem, Ga—, Sir Gavin. Let me know how you get on.'

Tuesday, 15 March 2022

Portillo rang to ask why, when he charged the phone, there were thirty missed calls and several death threats about some sort of double cross. I told him not to be so ungrateful.

Wednesday, 16 March 2022

Andrew Bridgen has withdrawn his letter of no confidence in the PM. Despite having zero faith in him only last month, he now believes that it would be wrong to get rid of a prolifically incompetent leader at a time of extraordinary global tension. He's right. Imagine if we'd done that in May 1940.

In other news, Thérèse Coffey is pregnant.

Thursday, 17 March 2022

Spring Conference. Road-tripped up to Blackpool in Matt Hancock's divorce Subaru with Michael Gove, James Cleverly and the Crabbmeister.

Just after Coventry, news broke that P&O had sacked 800 British crew. The shock sent Matt veering onto the hard shoulder. I had to grab the wheel and steer us back over the rumble strips to safety.

'But that means the shareholders at their parent company DP World must be in big trouble,' gasped Mike.

'And if they can't rehire some Indians on £1.80 an hour …' The Crabbmeister stopped mid-sentence as the realisation of what he was about to say hit him.

'Then they won't be able to afford to sponsor the European golf tour,' said James.

I said, 'Isn't it funny to think that only yesterday Boris was talking to the people who own DP World in Dubai.'

We sat in silence, contemplating the gravity of a situation in which Ross Fisher and Henrik Stenson might no longer be competing for weekly purses of a million pounds plus. Luckily, eternal optimist and most pompous man on earth James Cleverly was with us.

'Come on, guys, look on the bright side. If they do manage to shaft these workers then it's market capitalism, red in tooth and claw. And let's face it, that's why we all got into politics.'

'Yes, Jim, you're right,' I said. 'In fact, when you think about it, it's a good job Boris didn't do anything or else all these grasping seafarers might still be in a job.'

'Exactly, Secret,' said James.

'Hell yeah,' said Mike, who was now racking up lines on the Dover page of our *RAC Road Atlas* in the P&O shareholders' honour.

'Fucking aye!' yelled Matt, banging his red steering wheel paddle-shifter extensions, which caused us to swerve into the path of a speed-limited Stobart that had been trying to pass Matt's fuel-economy-focused 59 mph for several minutes.

It held down its horn. The Crabbmeister retaliated by bawling 'Spring Break' out of the window, skulling a Castlemaine, cracking the empty can on his head and throwing it at the wagon.

The Stobart pulled in front of us with half an inch to spare, forcing Matt to slam on the brakes. I turned up Starsailor on the stereo and James pulled out a dog-eared copy of *Britannia Unchained*.

'The Tory New Testament,' Matt murmured reverentially, unfazed by a windscreen full of Cumbrian HGV.

'The evangelists: Raab, Truss, Patel, Skidmore and Kwarteng,' shouted James.

'Go on, James, read us a bit and let's really get this party started,' said Matt.

James cleared his throat. 'The market must always be satisfied whenever and wherever it is encountered. British workers are among the worst idlers in the world, and the only way to hammer some sense into them is by shafting them, by either (a) working them harder for less money, or (b) replacing them with robots or something.'

We cheered, carried away by the poetry and cocaine.

'Matt, floor it,' ordered the Crabbmeister.

'What about my fuel economy? I'm on 37.6 mpg,' Matt replied.

Mike had the answer: 'You heard Chris Skidmore's silken prose; you only live once.'

'Oh, what the heck,' said Matt, dropping to third and shooting his Scooby back out around the Stobart. We pressed ourselves to the passenger-side windows, triumphantly wankering the incandescent driver.

We'd had an open invitation to Scott Benton's Blackpool 'layabout walkabout' to see what the dregs of society got up to in this part of the world, but after dragging an incoherent Crabbmeister past the landlady of our B&B and wrestling him into the recovery position in the bath, none of us really had the energy to go looking at tramps in the same state. So we got comfortable and watched Dewbs and Co. on GB News instead.

Friday, 18 March 2022

Late start after bleaching the bathroom and missed the afternoon schedule due to meeting Brandon Lewis and Mike Fabricant in Knobby's Karaoke Bar.

They were buzzing because they'd watched *The Rock* in their Airbnb last night.

'That's Secret's favourite film,' said the Crabbmeister.

'Guilty. I've watched it forty times. One for every year my son's been alive.'

'It is an exceptionally good piece of cinema,' said James. 'That bit where Nicolas Cage says, "Do you like the Elton John song 'Rocket Man'?" I love that.'

'Yeah, and that bit where Tony Todd is like, "I don't like soft-ass shit," and Nicolas Cage says, "Well, I only bring it up because it's you. You're the Rocket Man," and then he fires a stinger missile at him that knocks him onto an exposed spike,' enthused Brandon.

'I don't like soft-ass shit,' mimicked Mike Fabricant in an American accent.

'That's you, you're the Rocket Man,' said Brandon.

'I like *Flubber*. Do any of you like *Flubber*?' asked Michael Gove, who struggles in male-bonding situations.

Mid-afternoon, Liz, Nadine, Priti, Thérèse and Penny arrived, and performed a meticulously choreographed triple-bill of 'Wannabe', 'Say You'll Be There' and 'Two Become One' as the Spice Girls.

Watching Liz stomp around singing, 'Zig-a-zig-ah', in a cheap imitation of the Geri dress I sometimes dream about her in, I felt very much as if I might be falling back in love with her.

Nominal Sporty Thérèse did a forward roll too, and while I was mildly concerned that she should be performing such an athletic contortion in her condition, I didn't feel it was my place to say so with father-to-be Sir Gavin looking on so proudly.

Afterwards, Baby and Posh were at the bar discussing banning Islam. Sensing his chance, shirt unbuttoned, suggestive St Christopher nestling in a thicket of grey chest hair, Brandon Lewis wrapped his arms round both.

'Penny, is that a ladder in your tights or is it a stairway to heaven?'

Penny blanked him and ordered a thirty-shot tray of Butterscotch Corky's.

'Nadine, are you on Wi-Fi? Because I'm totally feeling a connection.'

Nadine had a bottle of VK Ice smashed on the bar and

pressed against his throat quicker than you can say, 'Specific and limited way.'

'Sorry, sorry, sorry. I've got a copy of Article 16 over there, I'll just go and read it.'

By 9 p.m. pretty much the entire 1922 Committee and most of the Cabinet had found their way there, and there was a blissful togetherness moment as we all stood together, arms aloft, belting out Robbie Williams's 'Party Like a Russian'.

I'd nipped outside with Michael Gove to do a bump of coke off his Levelling Up lanyard and was enjoying watching the Crabbmeister and Matt Hancock try it on with a pair of University of Lancaster Young Conservatives, when I spotted Gary Barlow and Sol Campbell sauntering towards us.

'Shit. It's Gary Barlow. And we're singing Robbie Williams. Mike, delay them.'

I struggled past the wall of whooping Tories that had formed around Dominic Raab, who was Cossack dancing to the music, and wrenched the sound system plug from the wall. This caused a predictably loud chorus of well-lubricated boos, but once Lucy Allan and Joy Morrissey had stopped spitting at me, I was able to warn them just in time.

'So – this is where the Shropshire North crew are hiding,' said Gary. 'Sol and I were wondering where everyone was for "A New North: How Can We Level Up Our Regional Economy Through Transport Investment?"'

'Yes, sorry, we got side-tracked,' I replied. 'Any good?'

'Legendary,' said Sol.

'Don't tell me you missed the "Data & Financial Compliance Best Practice" session too?' asked Gary.

'Sorry, no, yes,' I said, trying to pull my mind back into the zone while simultaneously hocking some lingering gak snot down my gullet.

'What have you been doing all afternoon?' asked Sol.

Before I could answer, Thérèse Coffey sashayed into our huddle and began grinding her hips into Gary. She was closely followed by Sir Gavin, who dragged her into the street.

'You're embarrassing yourself,' he started.

'Gavin. Gavvy poos. Chips and Gavy,' she said, spilling a pint of something blue and full of umbrellas down her chest.

'Sir Gavin.'

'Shir Gavvy Poos.'

'You shouldn't be drinking in your condition.'

'What condition is that, Gavvy? Give your Princess Leia a kish.'

He began trying to drag her away and she began resisting. I saw Sol about to intervene.

'Sol, no. Leave them to it. There's a code. What happens at conference stays at conference. And never get involved in anyone else's business, even if what they're doing is clearly wrong.'

Sol looked at Michael who nodded solemnly. Nadine and Penny came out next, presenting significantly more cleavage than during their rendition of 'Two Become One'.

'Gary, would you like to torpedo some Smirnoff Ices with us?' asked Penny.

He put his arms around the pair. 'Sure, and while you're here, I was wondering: are you girls a couple of loans? Because you've got my interest.'

They collapsed into fits of giggles.

Liz followed, walked straight past me, and began clumsily twiddling Sol Campbell's Union Flag bow tie before pointing at her own cheap sequin dress.

'Snap,' she said in her insipid voice, too drunk to remember to try and sound like Mrs Thatcher. 'Would you like to drink a WKD Blue really quickly with me, Sol?' she asked, demonstrably lacking her friends' most-popular-girls-in-the-fifth-form energy.

'No, Liz, I'm teetotal, but if you've got a minute, I would love to talk to you about data compliance. I've got so many questions.'

'How big is your majority, Penny?' Gary was asking.

'Fifteen thousand,' she said, putting her hand on his crotch. 'Nowhere near as big as yours.'

'Don't be so fockin' coarse,' snarled Nadine, smacking Penny's hand off his groin. 'Gaz la, when you've torpedoed these VKs you should come and sing us a song.'

'Can you even sing, Gary?' slurred Brandon Lewis while pissing against the back of a chip van.

'Brandon, don't speak to Gary Barlow like that,' I said.

'The man who lost us Shropshire North because he's shit

at press-ups?' said Brandon, who was now staggering towards us with a visible wet patch on his white chinos.

'Of course I can sing,' snapped Gary.

'That's not what I've *heard*,' said Brandon, who was laughing at his own joke even though nobody else was. He staggered around in a semi-circle. 'Idiots.'

'Six Ivor Novello awards says otherwise,' said Gary, patting the respective arses of the ministers for Digital, Culture, Media and Sport and Trade Policy in a calculated act of provocation.

'Brandon, that's enough,' I said again.

'Fuck you, Secret. You're just a shit Mark Francois. Oi, Barlow, do you like the Eric Clapton song "Rocket Man"?'

'That's an Elton John song.'

'No, you're supposed to say, "I don't like soft-ass shit".'

'Well, if you mean, "Do I like the Elton John song 'Rocket Man'?" then yes, I do.'

'Twat. That's you, you're the Rocket Man,' said Brandon. He then picked up a white patio chair and tried to hit him with it, but seventy-three-cap England international Sol Campbell was alert to the danger and removed the furniture from his grasp, steered the Secretary of State for Northern Ireland to the floor, put the chair on top of him and sat on it. Then he patted his lap.

'Come here, Liz, and tell me more about GDPR.'

'Gary, in here,' shouted Mike Fabricant in a Rasta dread-lock wig. 'Everyone wants to sing "Take That and Party".'

'Oh, I don't know about that,' said Gary modestly.

'I'll do it,' said the immobile Brandon from beneath the chair.

'No, no, I'll do it – *I'll* do it,' said Gary.

We walked in and Gary read the name above the DJ booth.

'DJ Trev, please can you do the honours? I'm Gary Barlow and I'd like to lead my friends in a song.'

Saturday, 19 March 2022

Woke up in bed next to Priti Patel. She was muttering into her phone: 'Send a team round to pick me up. Now. I don't care, wake them. I need exfiltrating.'

'Morning, Priti,' giggled Michael Gove and James Cleverly from the twin beds opposite.

'Morning, Priti,' groaned Stephen Crabb from the bath.

'Is that the Home Secretary?' asked one of the Lancaster University Young Conservatives who was drinking white Russians made with UHT from the tea service with Matt Hancock.

'Yes, or as I like to call her, the Pritster,' said Matt.

'Nobody calls me that,' snapped Priti, 'least of all you, you shit Richard Hammond.' She looked around. 'Urgh. Why are there more people than beds in here?'

'I was supposed to be top and tailing with the Crabbmeister but he keeps passing out in the bath,' I said.

'And the divorce is costing more than I expected,' said Matt, 'so I'm just sleeping on the floor.'

'Ms Patel, is it true you once singlehandedly deported fifteen Eritreans?' asked the other Young Conservative.

'Sixteen,' smirked Priti. She rolled over and I caught a glimpse of a back tattoo: *FACE ME FACE DEATH* in four-inch gothic lettering above a terrifying skull in a beret and a dagger dripping blood.

A knock on the door.

'Everyone turn around.'

There was a flurry of getting-dressed activity followed by a door slam.

'Get in there, Secret,' squeaked Michael Gove.

'Absolute lad,' said Matt Hancock.

'No way? Did you? Really?' asked a put-out James Cleverly.

I had no idea. 'One hundred per cent.'

'You were both comatose when we came back,' said one of the Young Conservatives.

'Yeah, that's because of all the fireworks,' I said uncertainly.

She turned back to Matt. 'So where do you get your black turtleneck pullovers from?'

His phone rang. She passed it to him: 'Gina.'

'Oh, sugar honey iced tea,' said Matt. 'She knows I need space to find myself. Why is she trying to contain me when I just want to fly free?' He threw the phone under the bed.

'OMG, did you just do that?' asked the wide-eyed young woman.

'Nobody puts Matt Hancock in the corner, Poppy,' he replied with a daredevil air.

'Saffy.'

'Whatever.' He casually ran his fingers around the collar of the polyester-mix pullover. 'Jacamo, I've got a sponsorship deal.'

We made our way to breakfast at the Winter Gardens, thrillingly pepped up by David Davis using the breakfast sausages to demonstrate how he thinks the latest Irish border might work. Colleagues in various states of dishevelment – Mike Fabricant with his wig slightly off centre, Brandon Lewis with a black eye, Penny Mordaunt with two black eyes, Liz Truss with a rosy glow – gathered around the halogen as he explained the intricacies using anaemic tubes of offal.

David's exposition was riveting, but I was feeling rather underslept so I made my way to trap two in the gents for a bit of me time.

The next thing I knew I was waking up to a call from The Saj saying Boris was on stage delivering the keynote speech. I'd been asleep for three hours.

I ran out without washing my hands, which is OK now because Covid is over, and through the first door I saw, which was a miscalculation, because it brought me onto the stage. Shielding my eyes from the spotlights, I found I was directly in front of Boris, who was woofily equating Ukraine's struggle for survival with Brexit.

After a lot of booing from my colleagues, presumably

directed at the G4S drongos manhandling me off it, I went and sat next to The Saj, who was enthusiastically patting a seat he'd saved me.

'You've got a piece of toilet paper stuck to your face,' he whispered.

Sunday, 20 March 2022

Spent the morning dealing with the fallout of Matthew and Stephen's decision to hotbox our bathroom with an ounce of some adulterated-to-the-point-of-not-being-illegal-any-more squidgy black they'd bought off a man with one leg in McDonald's toilets. Gratefully accepted Tom Tugendhat's offer of a ride home in the One Nation minibus. It used to be a double-decker executive, but they've had to downsize.

I saw Priti as I was checking out and tried to go and talk to her, but before I could I was intercepted by Chris Grayling, who had only just arrived at Conference having misread the dates.

In contrast to the outbound journey, the ride home was much more civilised, with the likes of Nicky Morgan, Caroline Nokes and Tobias Ellwood making polite conversation over coffee and pastries while watching Marr on a mini-TV at the front of the bus.

Rishi was on, saying that Boris hadn't equated Brexit and Ukraine yesterday and we'd all imagined it, which could have been true if it wasn't a lie.

Then, to take their minds off the direction the party is going in, we watched a palate-cleansing double bill of *Love Actually* and *The Wedding Singer*.

It was a pleasant change of pace from coughing in a cramped bedroom full of middle-aged men having panic attacks, although I can't pretend I wasn't a little jealous when Michael rang to say that despite having had no sleep, 'The lads were embracing Bolivian and driving to the Wirral for an afterparty.'

I could hear the others roaring with laughter in the background, as Michael giggled manically: 'I'm racking up lines and holding all the credit cards, Secret. I'm holding all the debit cards too, Secret. Secret, I'm holding all the cards!'

Funny thing happened when I got home too. There was a pig's head in my bed with a note in its mouth:

Does your moss-covered queen like Novichok?

'I've no idea,' I muttered to myself, before I kicked it onto the floor and went to sleep.

Monday, 21 March 2022

Someone from Boris's team told *The Times* that Boris was sorry for saying the thing about Brexit and Ukraine that Rishi had said he hadn't said, but that he wasn't going to apologise for saying it as he hadn't said it.

This is current Tory Party comms to a T: admit, deny, apologise, double-down, then whenever someone asks you about it, refer them back to whichever answer is most expedient.

Tuesday, 22 March 2022

Voted on Priti's Nationalities and Borders bill again – criminalising refugees, offshore processing, making it harder for people to prove who they are, generally pulling the already-just-out-of-reach ladder further away – all that stuff. We're pretending it's just for bombed-out Syrians and Yemenis, and not the Ukrainians, but that's just a bluff. We'll see how keen those guys are to come here after they've spent eighteen months battling Home Office bureaucracy.

Wednesday, 23 March 2022

Rishi did his spring statement today. It offered precisely nothing to the nation's poorest while dropping another 1.5 million below the poverty line.

Helpfully, despite their large number, none of these people actually have a place in our national discourse, which makes it awfully easy not to feel guilty about shafting them.

Afterwards, Rishi tried to win hearts and minds by doing a photoshoot where he filled up someone else's Kia Rio at a Shell and failed to use his debit card correctly to pay for it.

He was a bit upset when it didn't work and everyone laughed at him instead. He rang me afterwards to say that he now wished I hadn't put down Nova. I told him that if he needed another dog to make himself seem normal again, then he should call in at John Redwood's illegal puppy farm.

Thursday, 24 March 2022

Got interviewed on local radio about the budget.

They pulled that predictable stunt of asking me the prices of various household items to try and catch me out, so I was kicking myself for not bothering to find any out.

Having been stealing my lunches for the best part of a year and tasking Portillo to do my food shops online, I only ever really meet the price of things at service stations, where they're artificially inflated because you're paying for the experience.

Hence, when I said that a pint of milk was £2.50, a can of coke was £1.80 and a loaf of bread was £3, they were keen to hear how I expected people on £59 a week Universal Credit to get by.

'Quite easily. There are all sorts of things the poor and lazy can do to tighten their belts, from giving up their Netflix subscriptions, downsizing their estate cars and going on cookery courses with Lee Anderson, to registering themselves as non-domiciled for tax-dodging purposes. The sad truth is, too many of these people are giropractors, manipulating the benefit system for their own ends while refusing to sacrifice two weeks' skiing in Italy for one in France. And by the way, if your researcher wanted to go and price check these items at Birchanger Welcome Break, she'd find I'm not quite as detached from reality as you seem to think.'

'She?'

'It's not going to be a bloke in a junior role like that now, is it? Now give your listeners what they want and ask me about all the NLAWs we're sending to Ukraine and play "She Sells Sanctuary" by The Cult.'

Friday, 25 March 2022

Portillo is very stressed. There's been a spate of new graffiti. He demanded I come in to inspect a huge *Z* that's been done on the front door, the same logo Putin's been using to brand his backfiring special military operation in Ukraine.

He was in a real tizz. 'Dad, I think we're being deliberately targeted and it's in some way related to the death threats I've been getting on my birthday phone.'

'Listen, son, if people think I'm in bed with the Russians, then that's excellent PR because it means they think I'm a senior Tory. Ooh, look. I knew it. Whoever does the *SCUM* ones has had to buy a new spray can because that one is a luminous green rather than red. I bloody knew they were running out. They've had a slow start this year. They'll have their work cut out to beat last year's thirty-six.'

Saturday, 26 March 2022

A pub in Devon has renamed its ploughman's lunch a ploughperson's lunch. Like every other grifting cynic who revels in stirring synthetic culture wars, I am livid.

Sunday, 27 March 2022

After their release from captivity in Iran, there were big interviews with Nazanin Zaghari-Ratcliffe and Anoosheh Ashoori in the Sunday papers. I was kicking myself. If only I'd remembered to mention to somebody at the Foreign Office that I still had a constituent stuck over there, perhaps we could have got her out too.

Monday, 28 March 2022

Extraordinary drama at the Oscars. Will Smith hit Chris Rock because he did a joke about Jada Pinkett Smith's hair, which she keeps shaved because of alopecia. Will walked up on stage, said, 'Get my wife's name out of your mouth,' and slapped him. It's all anybody is talking about. Which works for us, as it's stopped everyone talking about the cost-of-living crisis.

Tuesday, 29 March 2022

To draw a line under Partygate, we had a lavish jamboree at the Park Plaza hotel.

Gyles Brandreth did the PA and put paid to any incipient party pooping with his belting opening line: 'I'm Gyles Brandreth and I'm going to talk at you in an unfeasibly self-satisfied way for two hours. Now, I know a few of you are worried about the optics; I'm here to tell you that the only optics that matter tonight are the vodka ones.'

It was great fun. The only downer, a 'Bereaved families of Covid' picket at the entrance. Most of us blanked them, but you can't hold back the irrepressible Mike Fabricant, who chucked them a super-recycled Brexit zinger: 'You lost them, get over it.'

Wednesday, 30 March 2022

First time showing sixth formers around the Palace of Westminster since the incident with Bill Cash's false teeth.

Burdened with the tedious worldliness that plagues well-taught A-level students, they wasted all of our time by challenging me on my voting record and asking why I was backing a demonstrable liar like Boris Johnson.

So I tried to bring a bit of levity to proceedings, showing them how to get free Quavers out of the vending machine by flicking the plug off and on, but they weren't impressed. Especially when the fuse blew.

'Jeremy Bentham said that it is the greatest happiness of the greatest number that is the measure of right and wrong, and we do appear to be having a rubbish time,' said a boy with a bow tie and acne.

'Yes, his behaviour raises some very problematic questions about Burke's trustee model of representation too,' said a girl with a shaved head.

'Maybe we ought to call the Met?' said a boy with spiky hair.

'Yeah, CSI Westminster, where they never solve a single crime,' said a girl with a nose stud. They all started laughing.

'You'll be laughing on the other side of your annoying faces when you've got a divorce, two mortgages and an SUV to worry about,' I yelled, before storming off and leaving Portillo to show them out.

Thursday, 31 March 2022

The siege of Kyiv has lifted. The Russians have left behind the sort of stomach-churning genocidal scenes that we had presumed, for no reason whatsoever, were over. It's taught us Tories a sobering lesson: when you are mollifying malevolent tyrants and sanitising the reputations of their malign operatives, do it discreetly.

April 2022

Friday, 1 April 2022

Bill Wiggin, Chair of the Committee of Selection, grilled Boris about why Qataris and Ukrainians (the right type of immigrants) are struggling to get into the country ahead of Syrians and Somalis arriving by dinghy (the wrong kind). It was a masterstroke from the Herefordshire stalwart: recalibrating his prejudices to look like they were about boats rather than skin colour so that nobody would notice he's a massive bigot.

Saturday, 2 April 2022

Went with Prince Andrew to a dogfight at John Redwood's illegal puppy farm. A nice chance to unwind after a tough few weeks at work.

There were some super bouts. Scrooge and Spock, Staffies belonging to Thérèse and Gavin, stronger than ever after their Blackpool wobble, bit lumps out of each other, while Lucy Allan's Rottweiler Myra (Hindley) tore the Corgi that Prince Andrew had entered in two. Andy was a bit sheepish afterwards, as he'd told the Queen he was only borrowing Philip.

The standout fight for me, though, was between Snowy and Erdogan: Michael Gove's Bichon Frise versus Chris Chope's Labrador.

As fourth-rate fifth columnist James Delingpole gathered dog organs in the background, I congratulated Snowy's victorious owner.

'That was first class, Mike, really top drawer.'

'Thank you, Secret, that means a lot,' he said nasally because his strapping young aide was stemming a nosebleed for him with a dog-poo bag.

'Any more panic attacks since Conference?'

'Just a couple. Nothing as bad as when I was married to Sarah.'

'Hello there, little Snowy. I remember when you used to be white,' I said, stroking the dog's blood-matted fur. Michael's aide took him from me proprietorially.

'Wasn't he yours and Sarah's, Mike?'

'Yes, but I had to take him off her. You heard about the Collies the RSPCA seized last month?'

'I had heard something.'

'It's very sad, completely malnourished and beaten to within an inch of their lives. Had to be put down in the end.'

'It's brought back some tough memories for us,' said the aide.

'Yes,' snivelled Mike, visibly reliving a couple as his assistant wrapped a large protective arm around him. 'I'm just glad I got this little guy out while I could.'

Another undoubted highlight was getting to speak to my hero Melanie Phillips.

Her pit bull Ariel (after the lefty Israeli not the Disney Mermaid) had just decapitated the unwanted Greyhound Matt Hancock got his children as a present for the affair he had, when she overheard me waxing lyrical about deporting asylum seekers. She stopped shrieking and asked if I'd like to go on the *Moral Maze*.

I couldn't believe it. At last, somebody has recognised my towering intellect.

Sunday, 3 April 2022

MP for Somerset and Frome David Warburton has been suspended following a £150k donation from an unscrupulous Russian, several allegations of sexual assault and a picture of him with a pile of white powder on an upturned baking tray. He has rebutted the allegations and claims the white powder was dandruff. You couldn't make it up.

Monday, 4 April 2022

It's full steam ahead with our plans to level up Britain: Nadine is getting rid of the overperforming, publicly owned and excellent-at-interrogating-Tories Channel 4.

Having asked us too many questions we don't like of late, it's going to be sold off for a billion quid. Nadine is saying that the channel isn't good value for the taxpayer, which is a bit weird because it's funded by advertising revenue, but who cares about that? Making it try to compete with Netflix has upset all the right people so we must be doing something right.

As sewage-outflow enthusiast George Eustice put it at lunchtime, 'We've got form when it comes to pumping out shit in streams.'

Tuesday, 5 April 2022

Matt and I were doing our Panini sticker albums in the kitchen at lunch when Priti walked in.

'Matt, could you give us a moment, please?' I asked.

'Sure,' said Matt, putting an upside-down sticker of Cristiano Ronaldo on the spot where a David de Gea shiny was supposed to go. 'I was just off to go and mix myself a Huel.'

'Give me my lunch,' ordered Priti.

I passed her sandwich bag of raw lamb kidneys from the fridge to her.

'I haven't seen you since conference, Priti.'

'I know that. Why are you telling me?'

'Well, I, er, I was just kind of wondering what happened really.'

'You guaranteed me the sex of my life, and because I'd had six Valium to take the edge off what happens inside my head, I agreed, but when we got back to your room you just sat on your bed quoting a film at me.'

'*The Rock*?'

'Yeah. You lured me there under false pretences.'

'Are you sure?'

'I'm certain,' she said, placing the heel of her stiletto on my left foot. I didn't dare make a sound. She took a wad of notes out of her white rhino leather handbag.

'I will let you make it up to me by taking this to William

Hill and putting a forecast on Noble Yeats and Any Second Now in the Grand National. I'm barred from all the bookmakers around here.'

On balance, I thought as I hopped around the kitchen clutching my toe afterwards, I'm glad nothing happened in Blackpool.

Wednesday, 6 April 2022

Nipped out to put that bet on for Priti when I was supposed to be scrutinising some data about children who've been left behind by the pandemic. It went smoothly apart from a minor hiccup when I inadvertently put her hundred-quid stake into a fixed odds betting terminal before I reached the till.

I've decided not to worry. There's more chance of Boris winning the Pride of Britain awards than her one-two coming in.

When I left I was surprised to see Steve Bannon, Andrew Bridgen, Steve Baker, Mark Harper and Des Swayne leaving the Costa Coffee over the road. As they said goodbye they all clicked their heels and saluted. Bannon shouted, 'Conservative Way Forward.'

Thought about asking what they were up to but couldn't be bothered. It seemed above board.

Thursday, 7 April 2022

Today's noise is about Rishi Sunak's multi-billionaire wife, Akshata Murty. She pays thirty grand a year for non-dom status to avoid paying twenty million a year in tax. Thirty k sounds a lot, but then I did the maths and twenty million minus thirty k is still twenty million.

Simon Clarke says Rishi rolled up the sleeves of his yellow cashmere cardi and spent the afternoon storming around the Treasury shouting, 'Take my wife's name out of your HMRC database.'

People are saying that having a chancellor whose family don't pay tax would be like having a third-rate influencer as Foreign Secretary, a philistine as Culture Minister or a feckless coward as leader. But I'm proud of him. Just because he sets the tax rates everyone else has to follow, it absolutely does not mean people can come after the woman he shares a bed with because she doesn't.

And anyway, as the sycophants' sycophant Lord Moylan said to me as I vaulted the ticket barriers on our way into the Tube this evening, 'Secret, it's our moral duty to pay as little tax as possible.'

Friday, 8 April 2022

Found another pig's head in my bed. This one said:

Eat your chip and fish from your soggy marshes.

Couldn't be bothered changing the sheets in case it happens again.

Saturday, 9 April 2022

Portillo thinks I need to keep the constituency party onside before the local elections, so I went down to my local Conservative club to watch the Grand National.

I wasn't so sure I needed to – this is the Home Counties, my constituency is 99.6 per cent white (I think it might be higher – I've never seen one) and we've had full control of the council since 1914 – but I said yes to humour him.

I did my best to interact with the Toilet Seats as little as possible by arriving late, but that didn't stop constituency chair Mrs Miggins seeking me out and whispering in my ear, 'I've got your number,' like she always does.

I demanded Denman in the sweepstake, who didn't win because he died three years ago, but there was something very familiar about the names Noble Yeats and Any Second Now that came in first and second.

I couldn't place them for ages, then Priti texted asking when she could collect her winnings. I had to sit down.

Double-crossing Russian mercenaries is one thing. Owing Priti Patel ten grand is something else entirely.

I bought some time by telling her we'd have to wait a few days for the bookies to gather the cash. Then, despite Portillo's protests at my not staying to draw the meat raffle, I went home and sat rocking in my darkened living room.

Sunday, 10 April 2022

Kept a low profile for obvious reasons.

Got several calls from Portillo during an excellent *Countryfile* piece about how the driven grouse killing fields are the only thing that stands between us and climate Armageddon.

I ignored Portillo and instead rang Viscount Rapacity to ask how he'd got the BBC's cuddly countryside magazine to be more obsequious than ever about organised wildlife crime.

'Oh, that's simple, Secret. John Craven has a soft spot for Latvian girls dressed as livestock auctioneers, and he doesn't check his bedroom for hidden cameras.'

Monday, 11 April 2022

Woken from dreaming about Liz Truss as a sexy livestock auctioneer by the Burkes' sodding windchimes. Then I heard a door slam, an over-revving engine and the screech of car tyres. I peered out of the curtains and gasped as I saw Portillo lying in the road.

I shot up, threw myself down the stairs, sprinted into the kitchen, turned on the radio, filled the kettle, put a Pop-Tart in the toaster, visited the Aitken Suite, and went out to see if he was OK.

The Burkes were already there, plying him with essential oils and saying he needed to go to hospital, but a perfunctory look at the dislocated fingers on his broken arm reassured me that he didn't, and I told them to piss off while I sat him at my breakfast counter with a box of plasters and a SunnyD instead.

Apparently, he'd been watching *Ant and Dec's Saturday Night Takeaway* on catchup when a gang of Russians abducted him and took him to a warehouse on the A406, where he was interrogated by a bloke with massive fists about my double-crossing them with the Dissident Dossier. They then tried to ring me to come and get him, but I didn't because I was watching *Countryfile*.

'Dad, I'm so proud of you for standing up to them.'

'Yep.'

'I always knew you'd stand up for what is right eventually.'

'Yep.'

'There was no way you'd ever let those vile bastards interfere with the integrity of British politics.'

'Yep. That's what I said.'

'They told me to tell you that they'll still give you twenty grand if you give them the right disks, otherwise they'll kill me. Obviously I told them you'd tell them where to get off.'

'Well, I …'

'Dad, no: if you can stand up to them, so can I.'

'Son, I am pleased to hear you say that, but I'm afraid it's game over. They've backed me into a corner and forced my hand, and I think I've now got no option other than to hand them the dossier and accept the twenty thousand pounds.'

'And save my life.'

'And save your life.'

The molten strawberry Pop-Tart scorched the roof of my mouth. I lifted a two-day-old Nesquik to cool it and gave Portillo the coaster it was sitting on.

'What's this?'

'The Dissident Dossier. I've been using the disks as coasters. Can you hand it over to the Russians for me? Obviously I'd do it myself, but it's too risky for someone with my profile.'

'Of course, Dad. I'm so proud of you.'

Tuesday, 12 April 2022

The Russians didn't even transfer the money this time, they just gave Portillo a black and orange Gola holdall full of notes.

I did briefly feel a touch guilty about selling state secrets which could undermine the fabric of our democracy, but that didn't last long; I've got the money to pay off Priti now, and ten grand with which to do what I like.

Wednesday, 13 April 2022

Boris has flown into Kyiv for a walkabout photoshoot with President Zelensky. This war, while dire for the people reduced to hand-to-hand fighting and drinking from puddles, has been quite positive for Boris, as there is a direct correlation between the quantity of Javelins we're sending to Ukraine and his popularity in the polls.

Thursday, 14 April 2022

Fifty Fixed Penalty Notices have been issued to Boris and his staff for partying during lockdown when others were obeying/mourning/getting depressed.

He's a bit skint so I lent him a fifty to pay for it from my illegal Russian money.

The Cabinet issued some fulsomely generic messages of support, several backbenchers voluntarily humiliated themselves and Edwina Currie got impatient with the Bereaved Families of Covid and demanded they stop their self-indulgent grieving.

Whisper it, but I think that finally a line has been drawn.

Friday, 15 April 2022

Good Friday.

Nobody seems to have noticed the line. But if there's one thing Boris is good at, it is getting people to forget the last thing they were mad about by pissing them off with the next one. And everyone shut up about Partygate when he announced that we're going to end human trafficking from Africa by trafficking humans to Africa. Specifically Rwanda, from whom we accepted 100 per cent of asylum applications in 2020.

It's policy red meat bloodier than a Brexit pig cull, and even though the evidence says 78 per cent of people arriving by boat are eventually granted asylum, Labour dare not argue with us because a decade of Nigel Farage on every current affairs programme has convinced the nation that they're all malign bastards coming to leech off us. I know this ignores the evidence, but evidence never had to live next door to these people.

The 2019 intake are literally soiling themselves with excitement. The picked-last-at-PE support group – Benton, Clarke-Smith, Gullis – were gushing all over Facebook and Twitter. It's so great to see this energy in the party again. I can't remember any of us getting this excited about feeding starving kids.

Saturday, 16 April 2022

The Russian money has been burning a hole in my pocket – I think it might have been in contact with some chemical weapons – so I've treated myself to a break at the Solstice Business Park Holiday Inn.

This made sense, because it's on the way to the replica Vatican beneath Jacob Rees-Mogg's mansion in West Harptree, where he has invited me to an Easter Mass tomorrow.

I was halfway through explaining how the Environment, Food and Rural Affairs Select Committee is structured to the rapt hotel barmaid, when I got a text from Steve Baker saying that as I was in the area – he must have seen the selfie I tweeted at the entrance to the business park – he hoped to see me at the MEGAchurch Faith Healing event he's organising in Stowey at exactly the same time as Jacob's mass tomorrow.

Obviously my refined sensibilities prefer Jacob's high church pomp and popery – if I'm going to have my credulity stretched to its limit I'd prefer it done by dogmatic men in grandiose finery rather than dogmatic men with acoustic guitars. But Steve has been throwing his weight around recently and I really don't want to risk putting his well-trimmed nose out of joint.

Mercifully, I saw on the map that the events are close enough to each other for me to do the hilarious thing that happens in tired sitcoms and satirical diaries, where a happy-go-lucky chancer climbs in and out of windows between simultaneous dates.

Sunday, 17 April 2022

Easter Sunday.

Whatever Rees-Mogg's service lacked in Catholic guilt it more than made up for in pageantry. A congregation of siblings and the several hundred cousins who were their children were led in prayer by Jacob, modestly attired as the Pope, and his altar boy Iain Duncan-Smith.

Jacob was intoning the penitential rites with such sincerity you could almost believe he'd never seen a Conservative Party manifesto. I could have listened to him all day, but I had to show my face at Steve's thing too.

I sneaked out under cover of incense – IDS was enthusiastically swinging a G4S-branded thurible around his head like a Romanist steer-ranching a herd of contraceptive-obsessed cattle – and drove up the A368 to the Folly Farm team-building complex.

The contrast was stark. *Express*-reading caravanning and swinger types and their teenagers in MEGAchurch merchandise, all listening intently to Pastor Steve in a pair of tiny denim cut-offs, neon Choose Life vest and dangly crucifix earrings.

'… And to those teenage members of the God Squad who thought it was funny to detune my acoustic guitar before I played "Puff the Magic Dragon" in front of the Pastor of Princes Risborough, I say you must be compelled to atone, to which I will personally see in my dressing room after this service. Breakout space three. It's very hot, so you won't need to wear much. Amen. And now we will sing "Faith" by George Michael.'

He put on a red MEGA baseball cap and slung a guitar over his shoulder.

I elbowed some kids out of the way to make sure he could see me and bellowed, 'I gotta have faith' as piously as I could on the chorus.

Steve stopped abruptly. 'Oh, day of days, a stray lamb. I believe Christ has presented us with a stray lamb.'

'A lamb, a lamb!' whispered the crowd.

'What?'

'Lamb, do you wish to be absolved of your sins?'

'What?'

'We wish to welcome you, lamb, into the fold. God created man in His own image, but that man sinned and incurred the penalty of death, physical and spiritual; thereafter all human beings inherited that sinful nature. Do you wish to be absolved, lamb?'

'Erm …'

'Is there a God-shaped hole in your life?'

'What? I don't … er … yes?'

'YES! It is time.'

'It is time, it is time,' chanted the crowd.

'For what?'

'For the laying on of hands.'

Everyone cheered. Steve played the opening chords of 1996 Britpop banger 'Place Your Hands' by Reef, as members of the congregation began babbling the kind of religious gibberish that you can't believe isn't a put-on.

Steve launched into a passable impression of idiosyncratic frontman Gary Stringer while, behind me, other members of the congregation began removing large reliefs of Elijah and Paul to expose a baptismal pool.

Steve pointed the headstock of his Fender at my solar plexus and nudged me backwards into the chlorinated holy water.

'I baptise you in the name of the Father and of the Son and of the Net Zero Scrutiny Group.'

'Put your hands on, put your hands on.'

'Put your hands on me.'

Discombobulated, spitting out water, coming to terms with my non-consensual baptism and noting that Steve was taking great care to navigate himself to the place where the maximum amount of hand putting-on could happen to his microscopic shorts, I swam to the edge where I was helped out by an overweight couple.

'I know you! You're bang on about the immigrants, you. Isn't he, Brian?'

'Bang on,' said Brian as he patted my hair with a King's Lynn Stars speedway towel that stank of dogs and cigarettes.

'We've got to look after our own. We have a lot at the end of our street, don't do anything. Tell him, Brian.'

'They don't do anything.'

'Just signing on and taking drugs. Brian?'

'Signing on and taking drugs.'

'So we just wanted to say, what you're doing with Rwanda – it's brilliant. No not like that, Brian.'

She snatched the towel and began rubbing me vigorously.

'Yes. It's the Christian thing to do,' I said. 'I really need to be going …'

'Yes, it is Christian, isn't it? Well, Mr Tory, if you're ever in Wisbech the kettle's always on.'

'Thank you,' I said, making a mental note never to go near Wisbech again.

I hurried back to Jacob's incense-fest, but the door had been locked. After a bit of rustling around, I found another entrance in the undergrowth behind a rusting Bentley and crawled down a long, low tunnel. *It's like* The Da Vinci Code, *this*, I thought to myself as I met a stone door with 'Pray for your moss-covered nanny' inscribed on it.

I think I must have been making a bit of noise because I could hear Jacob's larney consonants on the other side: 'Alleluia, Alleluia. It is an Easter miracle. Christ is here behind my stone door. Christ is risen, Alleluia. He is risen indeed, Alleluia, Alleluia.'

The stone slid to one side.

'It's not Jesus. It's Secret Tory,' croaked IDS.

'Oh, what is he doing in my priest hole? How very disappointing. I thought it might have been a miracle vouchsafed me by God as a reward for keeping all of my money offshore.'

'Sorry, Jacob, mate,' I said, pulling brambles out of my hair. 'Just me.'

'Well, come and sit down, Secret. I'm about to bless the petrochemical lobby in Latin.'

Monday, 18 April 2022

Bank holiday.

Spent the morning fly-tipping with Liam Fox, then went over to Priti's place in Witham to give her the money I got from selling state secrets to pay her back for the bet I didn't put on the Grand National for her. I won't lie, I'd rather have been watching James Bond.

'I only married you because we got overexcited working on the British American Tobacco gig in Burma, you worthless shit,' I heard her saying before she opened the UPVC door of her pebble-dashed seventies detached.

'Oh. It's you.' She thrust out her hand. 'Money.'

'Well done on Rwanda, Priti.'

Her dead eyes almost lit up. 'You don't think I'm being too lenient?'

'No, I think Rwanda is perfect. East into Tanzania would have been too lenient, west into the Democratic People's Republic of Congo a bit harsh. I think you've struck just the right balance. And, let's face it, they've come here for a better life so they deserve everything that's coming to them.'

'I know,' she smirked.

She also knew, without turning round, that a wretched man had emerged from the utility room.

'Who said you could leave that fucking room?'

'Nobody,' he whimpered.

'Are the shoes clean?'

'No. I wanted a drink.'

'You drink when I say you drink.'

The man skulked back into the utility room.

'Who's that?' I asked.

'Just a piece of shit I had the misfortune to marry ten years ago.'

She looked me up and down appraisingly. 'Are you single, Secret?'

'Er, yes,' I replied, taken aback.

'Right. I'll be in touch,' she smirked.

Tuesday, 19 April 2022

Caught Boris and Sue Gray having a meeting this afternoon. Boris was on a charm offensive, giving her all his best anecdotes – lying in front of the bulldozers, blowing the child maintenance in a casino, the bender with Evgeny Lebedev where he woke up with the Kremlin's automatic doors opening and closing on him – before explaining that if she decided to 'Back Boris' he'd give her anything she wanted.

Wednesday, 20 April 2022

Olly Dowden made us all go on a workshop run by spiritual catalyst Sir Edward Leigh called 'Dancing with the inner critic: colonialism as a systemic lens for engineering solutions based on the liberating stance of working within the fissures of a broken system'.

He did this by getting us to express ourselves with Play-Doh.

Matt Hancock made a little man with a pierced ear, leather jacket and babe on his arm who was driving an open-top sportscar away from a burning care home.

Dominic Raab made a musclebound man singlehandedly fighting off the Taliban with a paddleboard outside Kabul Airport.

Andrew Bridgen lodged his plasticine in his ear and had to go to hospital.

And I think I liked Andrea Leadsom's inner critic best. She made a little gunship attacking a dinghy full of refugees being captained by a man in a purple dress.

'It's the Archbishop of Canterbury getting sunk by the Royal Navy because he's a people trafficker who opposes our plans to deport funny-looking people to Africa,' she explained.

Thursday, 21 April 2022

Boris 'has been recalcitrant for only as long as he was in the headmaster's office, and his time is up'.

So sayeth Brexit hardman Steve Baker.

Everyone remarked on Steve's integrity in speaking out. And they're right to. Especially as his integrity tracks the modelling data that came out today saying he's on course to lose his seat.

Friday, 22 April 2022

Nadine has recorded one of these TikTok videos explaining that her role at the DCMS involves 'downstreaming tennis pitches so she can exercise her sport'.

The tolerant left had a field day laughing at this word salad.

It's so typical of them to go after her for something she can't help, like dyslexia, rather than something she can, like being a vindictive incompetent.

Saturday, 23 April 2022

St George's Day. Went and oversaw constituency celebrations at the Duke of York, a flat-roofed estate pub on the edge of town and easily the most patriotic hostelry in my constituency.

As I said to Portillo as we walked among the afternoon car-park drinkers, flaccid bunting, kids high on Fruit Shoots and a pair of plasterers fighting, St George's Day is often a bit samey.

I showed him a picture that West Dorset MP Chris Loder had just sent me from a primary school in his constituency. He was dressed as St George with his foot on the wrung neck of a white-tailed sea eagle that he was pretending was the dragon.

'We should do something like that, son,' I said.

'Where on earth did he get that poor bird?'

'Those busybody conservationists have been reintroducing them down there, so he's been out poisoning them with his shooting mates. What could be more English than that?'

Sunday, 24 April 2022

The *Mail on Sunday* has reported that Angela Rayner distracts Boris during PMQs by owning a pair of legs which she crosses and uncrosses like Sharon Stone in *Basic Instinct*. I texted Mark Spencer to find out if this was barrel-scraping misogynistic bullshit and he confirmed that it wasn't.

For example, if a male Tory MP had six, seven or eight children by different women, gave taxpayers' money to a pole dancer he was having an affair with, and deserted his wife while she was undergoing cancer treatment to shack up with another woman twenty years his junior, there's no way they'd let him rise as far as Rayner.

Still, I'm not happy with them for revealing our state secrets so easily. At least I got paid for mine. Imagine if our enemies knew that Boris was rendered inoperable by legs?

Monday, 25 April 2022

Literally nobody was up for it in our Defend the Indefensible WhatsApp group yesterday, so I was a bit cheeky and got Portillo to wangle me onto today's TV breakfast rounds. I'd be lying if I said I wasn't superb. Here are a few highlights:

April 2022

BBC Breakfast

Naga Munchetty: 'In the words of the respected constitutional historian Peter Hennessy, "Boris is sullying the offices of state like no other, turning it into an adventure playground for one man's narcissistic vanity." Are you not ashamed to come out in support of a man like that?'

Me: 'I think what you're actually asking me is do I think that the only way to build back better is by moving on from these stories about Boris inadvertently breaking his own laws while everyone else obeyed them and levelling up Britain instead, and I think the answer is yes.'

Naga: 'No, that's not what I'm asking …'

Me: 'Back off, Naga. You've seen what Nads is doing to Channel 4. Leave it.'

Sky Breakfast

Kay Burley: 'Your colleagues have been publicly jubilant about Home Office plans to deport asylum seekers to Rwanda, yet the Archbishop of Canterbury said that the plan "went against the nature of God". Does it not sit uncomfortably with you when the head of the Anglican Communion says you are at odds with Christ's message?'

Me: 'Did you just cross your legs? Are you trying to distract me?'

Kay: 'I absolutely did not.'

Me: 'I think you did. Anyway, where do these do-gooders get off calling me a hypocrite because the Bible makes an explicit case for welcoming strangers? It's disgusting.'

Good Morning Britain

Richard Madeley: 'Two hundred and sixty quid from Harrods, which I actually think is expensive, but you're paying for the quality.'

Me: 'Mine were twenty from Tie Rack.'

Madeley: 'OK, that's competitive.'

Me: 'They really are, Richard.'

Madeley: 'Susanna, where do you get yours?'

Susanna Reid: 'I don't wear cufflinks.'

Madeley: 'OK, after the break we've got the biggest dog in the UK, and he really is big – don't miss it.'

GB News

Eamonn Holmes: 'What I don't get, which happens a lot, in my head, is why we're talking about birthday cake and suitcases of booze when intellectually minded people like me got laughed at because we noticed the link between 5G phone masts and Corona.'

Me: 'You know what the MSM are like, Eamonn. They'd rather talk about fluff than focus on the rigorously researched theories of people sat on toilets scrolling Twitter. They're nothing but outrage archaeologists, raking through your past to look for all the times you've taken a bribe or had sex with a prostitute.'

Eamonn: 'I didn't know that was her job.'

Me: 'Things in the past are dead and buried. Like all the Covid people. Should we really be trying to make Boris take responsibility for his own actions when we could be amplifying the baseless theories of science-averse vloggers? I think not.'

Eamonn: 'Yes, I think if we start retrospectively punishing crimes, we're embracing oblivion.'

Me: 'Bolivian.'

Eamonn: 'Oblivion.'

Me: 'That's not a word.'

Eamonn: 'You know, Secret, I think this came up on *The National Lottery: Jet Set* once, and I really do think oblivion is a real word. But we leave no stone unturned here at GB News, so can we get the producers to do a fact check on that, please?'

Me: 'It's definitely Bolivian. I've never heard that other word.'

Eamonn: 'Yes, the producer is telling me oblivion is a word.'

Me: 'Oh. Well, Michael Gove told me that he was embracing Bolivian at Blackpool Conference. I wonder why he said that?'

Eamonn: 'My producer is also telling me that Bolivian means cocaine.'

Me: 'Right. Yes, that makes more sense.'

Tuesday, 26 April 2022

Elon Musk has bought Twitter for $44 billion. That's madness. I downloaded it for free on Google Play.

Wednesday, 27 April 2022

I was nipping over to my Hampstead Heath flat because I thought I ought to stash that bag of used notes the Russians gave me, when I saw Ed Miliband working out on the pétanque courts.

He was getting in the way of all the posh people between their visits to PT studios and blathering about skiing in delis, but he looked as tidy as he did back in December, if not more so.

I texted Gary Barlow immediately. He's going to have to do some serious training if he's coming back out on the campaign trail for the local elections next week.

Thursday, 28 April 2022

Did my first *Moral Maze*! Michael Burke's sonorous voice lent the proceedings a Bisto-like gravitas as we discussed the 'virtues of leadership', and wow, just wow, locking antlers with Melanie Phillips, Tim Stanley and Giles Fraser really tests your mettle.

Melanie's position was that proper leadership meant ending the UK's debauched and disorderly culture of instant gratification, feral children, violence and vulgarity on the streets; limelight-averse Giles gave an impassioned speech about his own experiences of being great; and high church spaniel Tim argued that an ideal leader was a jovial conman like Boris who we could all enjoy watching get out of scrapes. I felt compelled to support him, principally because it hadn't occurred to me to do any preparation, but also because treating politics like a game whose consequences don't affect me is a superb way of telegraphing that I've got a six-figure salary without being vulgar.

Friday, 29 April 2022

Huge day. The new vending machine has arrived in the lobby of Westminster Hall. Lee Anderson and I were inspecting it when we were ambushed by a group of struggling pensioners.

They were moaning about having to choose between heating their homes and eating, so I pointed them to Susanna Reid's interview with Boris this morning where he suggested keeping warm by riding around on a bus all day.

They were a surly lot. Not one of them was willing to

lend us the £2 coin we needed for a Brazilian Mango Mandarin Lucozade.

Saturday, 30 April 2022

Started door-knocking for the locals. Next door, to be precise, to ask the Burkes for their Wi-Fi code. Mine went down this morning when I remembered Angela Rayner has legs and accidently spilt my Vimto on the router.

They were at it too. From the moment Mrs Burke opened the door she was babbling at me about the cost of living and her electric doubling, as if I'm in some sort of position to do anything about it. Why is it that whenever anyone sees a legislator they start asking for help with their mediocre lives?

It really is a mystery. Anyway, I said the new thing we've been briefed to say, which is that Boris is going to build a nuclear power station every year for ever, but they didn't believe me because he can't even build a bridge, which to be fair to them is a good point, but I didn't want to admit that because I was still raging that their Wi-Fi password was Tran5W0menAreW0men.

May 2022

Sunday, 1 May 2022

First day of campaigning proper: a trip to the gym to prep Gary Barlow's pecs.

He's determined not to get shown up by Miliband again, so we went to Legends in Dalston because his body only responds to exercise stimuli when he's near other alpha males.

I was a bit out of my depth, if I'm honest; huge men wearing massive gold chains, yelling and throwing rusty weights on the floor really isn't my natural environment, but Gary seemed to know what he was doing:

He loaded up an already heavy-looking bar, asked me to spot him, pushed it up, yelled, dropped it on his chest and got pinned to the bench.

I released him with the help of a manager called Tyrone.

When he could breathe again, he laid into me, saying that it was all my fault and he can usually do that weight and I wasn't spotting him properly.

He's half-right. I wasn't spotting him properly. I don't even know what that is.

'How much do you usually lift?' Tyrone asked him.

'Two fifty.'

'Two fifty?'

'One fifty.'

'One fifty?'

'Eighty. It goes up and down.'

Monday, 2 May 2022

Early May Bank Holiday.

Portillo dragged me to Tory Teas on the Green, an excruciating stale-buns-and-racist-pensioners affair, to get my constituency party pumped up for the last week of campaigning.

It was made marginally tolerable by watching Elsie and Lucy's octogenarian peers treat them like royalty because they work closely with me. They plied them with sugary treats to find out if they ever got to go out shaming benefit cheats and cooed like semi-continent doves when they found out that I sometimes let the girls have a Garibaldi on a Monday.

There was also a bit of talc-and-lavender-scented clucking over a five-tier illusion cake of Gerald Nabarro that Lucy had made, and I was enjoying taking slices out of different sides to ruin it when I got Mrs Migginsed again.

'Secret,' she said in the stern voice she usually reserves for foreign delivery drivers, 'I will always vote for an unscrupulous Tory over a Trotskyist Lib Dem. But Boris's monkeyshines are having a severe impact on the doorstep. I want your personal assurance that your own personal conduct will not be compromising our 100 per cent Blue council.'

With the memories of what she did to those Travellers on the bypass last year still fresh, I assured her that I wouldn't be doing any letting down.

A short time later Lucy succumbed to a hyperglycaemic attack brought on by excessive dainty consumption. With the other cauliflower-heads running around in a mad panic, it was clear that the situation didn't need overcomplicating, so I sneaked out and drove home.

Tuesday, 3 May 2022

Keir Starmer is being investigated for having a curry with colleagues at a time when you weren't allowed to socialise with more than six people.

After weeks of tabloids regurgitating the line that Partygate isn't important because there's a war on in Ukraine (although I'm not sure that works because the logical extent of shelving one problem because a worse one exists somewhere else is that there is no real problem other than the worst one in the world), they've decided it does matter after all, and our client journalists Harry Cole, Dan Hodges and the proper weirdos at Guido Fawkes have stepped up to the plate and are making hay, demanding that Starmer resigns for being a smug git.

Wednesday, 4 May 2022

Amazing how life creeps up on you. It's local elections tomorrow, and I realised I still hadn't done any proper canvassing yet.

Gary came over first thing, and we were getting set with a power breakfast of a bowl of Sugar Puffs made with a can of Monster when I got a call from Olly Dowden saying CCHQ urgently needed the big guns to go and target a blue ribband electoral ward in West Wales.

I wasn't unsurprised to hear my exceptional skills were needed elsewhere. But after six hours on the M4 with Gary, Andrew Bridgen and Mark Francois, and an afternoon traversing the potholed bridleways of Cenarth and Llangeler, where everyone insisted on speaking Welsh unless it was to tell us that the last century has seen seventy years of Tory government that Wales never voted for once, and then discovering that the only people standing in the wards were Plaid Cymru, I couldn't help thinking our full potential wasn't being realised.

It was a long drive back, made marginally more bearable by watching the built-in headrest TVs in Mark's Evoque. We watched an episode of *The Simpsons* where Homer and some other idiots were given the pointless task of guarding a bee in a jar in the basement of the nuclear plant to get them out of the way during a crucial inspection. The plot resonated for some reason.

Thursday, 5 May 2022

Election Day. Despite what Mrs Miggins says, I can't imagine the cost-of-living crisis, the broken promises, the endemic sleaze, the 80 per cent of the public who think Boris is a liar, or the massive billboard posters outside the polling station that the local Labour group have knocked up of me loading a Corby trouser press into the boot of a Saudi Hummer will resonate.

Friday, 6 May 2022

We have lost control of the council. Nationally, we have been obliterated.

Mrs Miggins lost her seat to a nineteen-year-old Green with blue hair. She said she's going to do everything she can to bring me down. I told her I didn't care because I don't have to listen to her any more, but then Portillo explained that she's still the constituency chair and I do, so I apologised.

Everyone's fussing about Sinn Fein winning a majority in Northern Ireland, too. Dom Raab says it's the EU's fault because they've made us put a trade border in the Irish Sea, which was only supposed to go there over Boris's dead body, and if I'm going to get my expertise from anyone, it's from the man who didn't read the Good Friday Agreement when he was Foreign Secretary, even though it's only thirty-five pages long.

Brandon Lewis has invited everyone to Stormont House to try and settle things amicably over a cheese fondue. Like, who put that bloody border across the middle of Ireland in the first place?

Saturday, 7 May 2022

Popped into Halfords to talk about getting some integrated TVs installed in the headrests of the Overfinch, and ran into Thérèse and Gavin coming out of the Early Learning Centre.

'Hi, guys. What are you doing here?'

Thérèse pulled a half-smoked Café Crème from behind her ear and relit it. 'Shopping. We get recognised in our own constituencies.'

I nodded at their ELC bags full of wipe-clean eating apparatus and educational toys. 'Ah, lovely. Getting prepared?'

'What? Oh no, this is for Gavin, for when we move in together.'

'And how's the bump?' I asked, patting her tummy.

'All good, thank you, Secret. We've got the first scan in four weeks.'

'Yes, you are definitely starting to show.'

Gavin took my hand away and gently replaced it with his. They looked at each other dotingly. He turned back to me.

'You know that day you found us in the DWP store cupboard?'

'Yes.'

'Well, we think that's when it was conceived,' said Thérèse.

'Wow. So, presumably you'll want to name it after me. And that should be fine, subject to certain conditions.'

They stood in silence thinking about it.

'Secret Tory, you wanker!' shouted a passing truck driver, ruining the moment for all of us.

'Yeah why don't you fuck off?' I hollered after him. I turned back to the star-crossed lovers. 'I love the banter you get around here.'

Sunday, 8 May 2022

Starmer has said he'll resign if he gets a Fixed Penalty Notice. Which has rather backfired in the faces of the payroll journos whose livelihoods rely on tip-offs from Carrie about Boris. They've all gone into meltdown.

Alex Wickham ordered an extra strong spinach and kale smoothie, Paul Staines ordered an extra private school fop to do his dirty work for him and Harry Cole started tweeting, 'I can't help it, I still love her,' before driving to Number Ten to beg Carrie to come back to him.

After making him get down on all fours to eat a plate of Whiskas, she said no.

Monday, 9 May 2022

Yes, we might have been destroyed in the locals, and yes, the party might be in meltdown, but something much more important happened today.

I was in the kitchen watching Putin parade his nukes through the middle of Moscow, thinking we ought to do something like that in Milton Keynes, when Liz Truss walked in wearing a headscarf and a pair of shades, like Audrey Hepburn but with a tin of Del Monte Fruit Cocktail.

She's had a spring in her step ever since Blackpool Conference, like she's had some sort of awakening. She withdrew a pink tin opener from her Cath Kidston tote bag and brandished it in front of me.

'Well that's … uncanny,' she giggled.

'Yes,' I replied, noticing her tin was a ring pull. 'I was just looking for my Dairylea Dunkers, which is why I'm holding Grant Shapps's cocktail sausages.'

She paused for a moment and looked out of the window. Then she turned to me with pouting lips, narrowed eyes and a toss of her thin hair.

'Mmm. I like a nice big bit of pork,' she said with her customary adenoidal gravitas.

'Yes, so do I. In fact, I keep finding pigs' heads in my bed at home, but I must reiterate, I would never dream of eating Grant Shapps's cocktail sausages.'

'Oh, really? Well, I'd love it if you *slipped me one*, Secret.'

'Yes. I'll be. Sure. To do. That,' I replied in stunned staccato, as syrup from a piece of discoloured melon dripped down her fingers.

'Oops,' she said alluringly, fixing my eyes as she licked her fingers.

'Yep,' I faltered. She knocked over the can with her elbow and it fell onto her white trousers.

'Oh, shit. No, no, no, these are Jenny Packham.'

'Yes, well, that wouldn't have happened if you'd been paying attention.'

'But I'm supposed to be talking to the Ukrainian ambassador in ten minutes. Shit, shit, *shit*.' She ran out summoning Flo, Poppy, Char Char and all the other exorbitantly educated advisers responsible for helping her dress.

I was stunned. Had we been talking about Grant Shapps's cocktail sausages? Or had I just been flirted with by a Liz Truss with the confidence of Joan Rivers and the wit of Les Dawson?

Tuesday, 10 May 2022

Dreamt I was on a date in the Solstice Business Park with Liz, but with the head of a pig. It was strangely erotic until I noticed the pram next to us. Piglet twins with the heads of Gavin Williamson and Thérèse Coffey.*

I decided to ring Liz's best friend Anne-Marie Trevelyan to get some intel, and she kindly took five minutes out of a cream tea at Claridge's with her Russian donor friend Alexander Temerko to tell me that Liz is so immersed in her responsibilities at the Foreign Office right now that her eye has started twitching every time someone mentions another country, there's a trail of Baileys miniatures everywhere she goes, and last week she wore a playsuit from Primark to a meeting with the US Ambassador, which everyone agreed was a cry for help.

Wednesday, 11 May 2022

State opening of Parliament.

Her Majesty the Queen couldn't make it due to realising that, at ninety-six, life is too short, so her crown was driven to Westminster by a fleet of Rolls-Royces and Charles did it instead.

---

* Must remember to get rid of the pigs' heads on my bedroom floor. I stubbed my toe on one of them yesterday and the older one is beginning to turn.

State openings haven't been the same since coalfield quip-ster Dennis Skinner stopped heckling at them, so I thought I'd reinstate the tradition myself by shouting, 'You're just a shit Prince Andrew,' at Charles as he walked past. Mixed response.

Anyway, say what you like about the optics of one of the world's richest men sitting in a gold throne next to a hundred-million-quid hat delivering a speech that offered nothing to the seven and a half million people currently skipping meals. Yes, just say what you like about it.

Thursday, 12 May 2022

With Finland and Sweden set to join NATO, Russia has threatened us with its RS-28 Sarmat, a hypersonic nuclear missile they say could reach the UK inside 200 seconds.

It's quite incredible, I thought as I was taking out the bins, *that of the planet's 4.5 billion years, humanity is on the point of voluntarily making itself extinct after only 300,000.*

What an achievement that would be, the epoch-flouting equivalent of Mike Fabricant's fiftieth when Des Swayne got us kicked out of TGIs for pissing on the counter before we'd sat down.

Friday, 13 May 2022

When I alighted at Westminster Underground today I got pushed into an alley and thought I was getting mugged because of Sadiq Khan legalising knife crime. But it was Priti Patel.

She says she noticed some feelings for me when I gave her that cash, and that they must be special because she never has feelings. Then she said we're going to start having an affair.

I thought about Liz Truss with her syrupy fingers and wasn't sure I felt the same way.

'I'm taking your silence as assent. Sign this.'

'What is it?'

'An NDA.'

Remembering something Prince Andrew had said about NDAs being good for the start of a relationship, and because I was scared, I signed it.

'Right, I'll set up a shared diary for our fluid transfers. You can go away now,' she smirked.

Saturday, 14 May 2022

I've got a feeling I've made the wrong decision with Priti, which was compounded when I woke to a typo-ridden text from Liz Truss asking in what position I'd paint her on the nose of my Lancaster. It was a genuine dream come true. But I've literally just signed an NDA with Priti. I didn't know what to say so I replied with the classic politicians' fudge:

'Reclining sideways, suggestively cradling a bomb, FULLY CLOTHED.'

Sunday, 15 May 2022

It's my birthday. Portillo got me a Union Jack keyring, Elsie and Lucy gave me another badly knitted Michael Caine doll and Matt Hancock asked 1922 WhatsApp if anyone wanted to record a video message for me, but forgot I was in the group so I saw north of fifty messages telling him to fuck off.

I also got a call from Yevgeny Prigozhin, although that wasn't strictly birthday related as he was in the middle of a firefight in Donetsk and wanted to tell me that his Wagner Group had been relying on the atropine I'd given them at Stonehenge for when they were firing chemical weapons at civilians, and it wasn't working.

I tried to tell him that if he drank it, it would give him a tasty energy boost, and he told me that he was going to rip my head off and shit in the neck, so we agreed to disagree and catch up over a few beers when he finishes his special military operation.

I thought about telling my new girlfriend Priti but decided not to because of her personality.

Monday, 16 May 2022

On the *Moral Maze* again this evening.

After we'd solved gay marriage, Baroness Fox took me to one side and asked if I'd ever thought about joining a think tank. I tried to pretend it wasn't my longest-held ambition behind doing *Robot Wars*.

'Great, I'll be in touch,' she said in her homicidal Mercian drawl.

You never realise how much you want to be a faux-intellectual puppet of far-right financiers until someone asks you.

Tuesday, 17 May 2022

Rishi accused Grant Shapps of nicking his Innocent Smoothie from the staff fridge today. Grant denied it and called Rishi an overpromoted barista, and Rishi couldn't think of anything to say back so shoved him into a bust of Oliver Cromwell, which fell off its plinth and broke. Then they ran off.

Wednesday, 18 May 2022

The Met have now issued a mere 126 fines to Number Ten for parties during lockdown.

Despite this vindication of Boris's leadership, I got a message from Steve Baker impressing on me the importance of joining his breakaway faction Conservative Way Forward. I tried to tell him I've got his sodding groups coming out of my ears, the CRG, the ERG, the NZSG, now the CWF. But he didn't listen. Truth be told, I'm increasingly worried about associating with Steve. He's been telling people he's been getting Nigel Lawson stigmata wounds anointing him as the chosen one.

Thursday, 19 May 2022

With the cost-of-living crisis beginning to bite, we have been sending out our best and brightest to help the nation.

First up was Lee Anderson explaining that 2.5 million foodbank parcels were distributed last year because of a national decline in culinary aptitude, which is a lot of people losing their way around a kitchen since 2010 when only 40,000 parcels were distributed. Incidentally, that's also the year we came to power. Lee's solution is giving out food conditional on recipients going on courses that tell them how to cook it. And he's spot on. If we're giving it out for free, then what the paupers eat should be our choice, not theirs.

Then Jackie Doyle-Price said we should incentivise granny annexes so that young people can unlock the wealth in their parents' properties, a policy which will really resonate with the terraces of the north and Londoners in flats.

And, finally, we had Rachel Maclean, me neither, saying that poor people could protect themselves from rising prices by working more hours or moving to a better-paid job.

What more can we do? If they're getting advice like this on tap and still choosing to be poor then I'm afraid it's on them.

Friday, 20 May 2022

To commemorate inflation hitting 9 per cent we have unveiled a statue of Mrs Thatcher in Grantham.

Sadly, egg throwing began almost immediately.

Although then a man turned up and began selling eggs for people to throw, and I couldn't help thinking that she would have applauded his entrepreneurial flair.

Saturday, 21 May 2022

Nervous. First liaison with Priti tomorrow. Bought some bootleg Viagra off Brandon Lewis.

Sunday, 22 May 2022

'You're late, take your clothes off,' said Priti in our Waterloo Days Inn budget twin.

I stripped down to the Hurricane Y-fronts I got from the Imperial War Museum Duxford gift shop. She was unable to hide her displeasure.

'Oh, no. No, no, no. I didn't realise you looked like that.'

Having caught a glimpse of myself in the mirror, I could see where she was coming from. 'Sorry, Priti. I didn't think to mention that I was physically repulsive.'

She began hissing. 'What a waste of time.'

'Sorry, Priti.'

'No. Listen. That *GQ* tosser Johnny Mercer is doing bootcamps on College Green before the summer recess. I need you to get a six-pack by July, otherwise there will be consequences.'

'Yes, Priti.'

'I'll let you settle the bill, seeing as you lured me here under false pretences again. See you at the second reading of Chris Chope's amendment to the 1983 Mobile Homes Act. Don't make eye contact.'

'Goodbye, Priti,' I said to the slammed door.

Monday, 23 May 2022

I spat out my Sugar Puffs at breakfast. Jodie was on the radio. She'd rung Nicky Campbell to talk about the cost-of-living crisis, waffling on about all the times she'd had to choose between heating and feeding herself, and how she'd seen the other side of the coin on a shooting weekend where

Tories literally burnt money in front of her eyes. I texted 85058 immediately:

'Just because that woman can't budget a week's food off twenty quid doesn't mean she can denounce Tories for lighting cigars with fifties that they've earned by having bigger investment portfolios than her.'

Tuesday, 24 May 2022

The Sue Gray report has come out, and like Belshazzar's feast, the wine is on the wall. She has found that Downing Street staff brazenly discussed their lockdown parties, bragged about getting away with them, Boris attended eight of the sixteen parties, one Christmas party left Rioja on the walls, another had vomiting and a fight, there was a 4.20 a.m. finish on the day of Prince Philip's funeral when flags were flying at half-mast over Number Ten, there was photo evidence of a party Boris denied had happened, and cleaners and security staff were treated shamefully.

Not too bad, really. As Boris said afterwards, 'I've had worse reports.'

Wednesday, 25 May 2022

First day at Johnny Mercer's Golddiggas bootcamp.

Other than shooting sentient wildlife, I've never really done any sport, but from the moment Johnny greeted his unfit legislators, we were at ease.

There were lots of us there. The rougher lot, Scott Benton, Ben Bradley, Brendan Clarke-Smith, but old hands too like Dom Raab, Penny Mordaunt and Peter Bottomley, as well as lobby journalists Harry Cole, Nick Robinson and Peston.

It was tough. I almost passed out during the bleep test and didn't think I was going to survive the twenty-minute ab blast, but somehow I found a second wind when Johnny told me that 'pain is just weakness leaving the body'.

'You did really well today, bro,' he said afterwards, gently wiping some snot off my cheek.

I was thrilled. Nobody has ever called me bro before.

I texted Priti to tell her I'd done as she said, and she replied to tell me not to make contact again until I've hit 10 per cent body fat.

Thursday, 26 May 2022

Woke up with kidney failure. Every time I moved it made it a hundred times worse. It was so painful I had to ring Portillo to tell him he was going to have to flout his driving ban and get me to hospital, because there are no ambulances after twelve years of Tory government.

But he didn't answer, so I writhed in agony on my bed watching Grant Shapps being interviewed by Charlie Stayt, wondering if this is how it all ends.

I was in such pain that I even began hallucinating like Renton in *Trainspotting*.

One minute I was rooted in reality, gazing at the maggoty pigs' heads on my bedroom carpet. The next, a peal of celestial trumpets announced a choir of cherubs in Fila tracksuits singing 'You've got this, bro' to the tune of 'Zadok the Priest', which in turn heralded the appearance of an angel with the body of a white-tailed sea eagle and the face of Johnny Mercer that winked at me.

'Yes!' I shouted, boldly swinging my legs to the floor, pushing myself into a sitting position and taking a Wagon Wheel from the fruit bowl by my bed. 'I have got this.'

My phone beeped.

'OMG DOMS! Peston.'

'What?'

'It's an acronym, which is an abbreviation formed from the initial letters of other words and pronounced as a word. Peston.'

'I know what an acronym is. What's DOMS?'

'Delayed Onset Muscle Soreness. High-intensity exercise causes microscopic tears in your muscle fibres. Your body responds to this damage by increasing inflammation, which may lead to a delayed onset of soreness in the muscles. I find this stuff fascinating. I guess that's why I'm always asking questions. Peston.'

'I thought I had kidney failure.'
'No, you've got DOMs from doing loads of sit-ups. Peston.'
'OK, cheers Preston.'
'Peston. Peston.'

I breathed a sigh of relief, which I instantly regretted because my abs flared up again.

Friday, 27 May 2022

Took a second day off due to my sore abs and then wished I hadn't. After her stir on Nicky Campbell on Monday, sodding Jodie had been invited onto *Woman's Hour* to talk to Emma Barnett about her experiences of politics from the other side. I was so angry I threw my radio on the floor and broke it, which was doubly annoying because I listen on my laptop.

Saturday, 28 May 2022

There are no words. Just Stop Oil protestors have smashed up the petrol pumps at Clacket Lane Services. Imagine the entitled gall required to temporarily deprive SUV drivers of £1.99-a-litre Unleaded Supreme.

It's getting a bit much now, the growing number of people fussing about the planet's transition into unliveability. So I have made a promise to myself:

From this day forward, I will never, *ever* greenlight a wind turbine.

Sunday, 29 May 2022

The excellent Friends of Clacket Lane group on Facebook organised a spontaneous 'pump pals drive-out' in solidarity with BP.

The plan was to fill our tanks at Clacket Lane's westbound BP, drive a full circuit of the M25 in second gear to burn as much of it as possible, then return to refill eastbound.

I couldn't say no, so instead I said it to the Iranian Foreign Minister who wanted to offer some new concessions for the constituent of mine he's got hostage.

We assembled with an air of quiet resolve, steadfast petrophiles unwilling to let yesterday's desecration of this sacred site prohibit us from burning as much fossil fuel as possible before rising sea levels breach the Thames Barrage.

Many of us filled extra jerry cans. But it was Mark Francois who stole the show by towing a thousand-litre bowser with his Evoque. As he trundled away saluting, his poorly attached trailer sloshing two grand's worth of petrol across the forecourt behind him from the incorrectly closed cap, his spontaneous ovation was well-earned.

Afterwards I popped into WHSmith to look for Jodie to tell her what we'd just done and how unbothered I was about her going on the media all the time.

She was stacking a shelf of travel sweets. I went and gave her a light pat on the bottom to say hello, and was surprised when a woman who wasn't Jodie turned round and hit me.

After nearly convincing her that it was a mistake, she told me that Jodie left months ago. Apparently, she's become some sort of high-flyer and has got herself a job as a midwife.

I must have inspired her to improve herself.

Monday, 30 May 2022

Priti texted me a picture of Peter Andre in his 'Mysterious Girl' prime, telling me I have to look like that by July, so I popped over to Conservative peer Michelle Mone's house after work to get a pack of the bootleg diet pills that Steve Barclay swears helped him get a six-pack. I'm enjoying the bootcamps, but I think I'm going to need all the help I can get.

We were having a giggle about Tiverton MP Neil Parish watching tractor porn in public in the House of Commons again, when there was an almighty crash and the front door caved in.

It was the police, raiding Michelle's house for evidence related to her buying £46 million of unusable PPE from China which she then sold to the NHS for £122 million using the VIP fast lane.

It was very dramatic, and Michelle was crying. But after I explained to the police that I barely knew her, definitely wouldn't testify for her, and that I was only buying the illegally manufactured pills for a friend who is a volunteer Samaritan, they let me leave.

Tuesday, 31 May 2022

Met Matt Hancock in the St Stephen's Hall lost property office. He was beside himself. He said that at one point last month he'd poured a litre of Innocent Smoothie labelled 'R. Sunak – billionaire' straight down the sink just for the thrill of it.

I nodded and showed him a Babybel. 'These are Kit Malthouse's. I don't even like them.'

It felt good to open up. We agreed it had gone too far and had to stop. I suggested we swear on the grave of Eric Pickles, but Matt pointed out that Eric isn't dead yet because he went for lunch with him last week, so we swore on the grave of Dennis Thatcher instead. I suspect we didn't choose Maggie because, deep down, we wanted to keep our options open.

June 2022

Wednesday, 1 June 2022

More talk of leadership elections after Andrew Bridgen resubmitted his letter of no confidence in Boris, but off the record Graham Brady confided that any challenge was unlikely because Andy had given him his car-insurance renewal by accident.

In other news, Jodie has now been on *Loose Women*. How come she gets to rub shoulders with Denise Welch before me?

Thursday, 2 June 2022

Her worshipfulness Queen Elizabeth the II of Great Britannia, Ireland and Wales has reigned over us for seventy years.

An era which started in the fifties with austere living, unheated houses, rationing and far-right anti-immigration rhetoric is ending as it begun.

Beacons have been lit up and down the country. In my own constituency a group of children with learning difficulties were going to light one in the Jubilee Park. They had been practising for seven months and were very excited about it, but I am a massive fan of the Queen so I instructed the organisers to cancel them because I wanted to do it instead.

They tried to object, but when I told them I was a member of the Oligarch Sanction Taskforce and it was within my power to sanction their Variety Club minibus off them, their carers agreed.

The ceremony itself was quite fun and I made sure we did it in front of my new dogshit bins, although having cancelled the special kids and their proud entourages, the audience of two – a photographer from the *Advertiser* and a health and safety man dressed in fire-retardant clothing called Clive – did leave the twenty-acre park feeling a touch empty.

Friday, 3 June 2022

Read at breakfast that Everton had been invited to the Queen's Platinum Jubilee Thanksgiving service at St Paul's on the strength of the Victoria Crosses he won in the Falklands and Operation Desert Storm.

There was no way I was letting him upstage me like that, so I got straight on the phone to Prince Andrew and got him to swing me a last-minute invite.

After a quick shower and change into some cream chinos and a salmon pink Henri-Lloyd, I headed for town.

There was a bit of a kerfuffle at the Great West Door when I arrived. Mike and Zara Tindall were arguing with the security services about not being allowed in. Andy whispered that this was because he'd bumped them off the guest list for me.

He arranged for me to walk right behind the party leaders, too. I've always wondered what these public adversaries discuss on such occasions. Who won the last PMQs? Living standards? Ukraine? Persistent lawbreaking? So I scuttled along, trying to eavesdrop.

'Is the new vending machine in the Jubilee Cafe still broken?' Boris was whispering.

'Yes. I put a £2 coin in yesterday and it didn't give me a Mars bar or change,' honked Keir in his funny voice.

'Drat. I had the same thing with a Bounty, which was jolly embarrassing because I'd already had to ring one donor to come in and buy it for me.'

'One-fifty a Twix; don't they know about the cost-of-living crisis?'

They both laughed. I pushed my head between them.

'Lads, if it's like the old one, if you go to the plug socket and turn it off and on at the right speed, it makes all the motors go, which then pushes one of everything out at the same time.'

'Really?' they said simultaneously.

'Yes, but the plug is behind the machine, so you must lie on your belly and reach under to do it. So ideally there needs to be two of you, one to do the switch and one to watch it's working. Me and Lee Anderson filled a carrier bag with Quavers, Maltesers and Fruit Polos after PMQs last week.'

A member of the security services put a firm hand on my shoulder and pulled me back.

'Want to try it, Keir?' joked Boris.

'A moment of unity could look good for both of us,' dork-tificated Keir.

I sped up again. 'I'd probably need to be there too to show you how to do it.'

The security man grabbed me again and pushed me into a pew next to Theresa May. I offered her a Malteser but she turned away haughtily. Boris and Keir sat in front of us.

'Boosts?' whispered Keir over his shoulder.

'Everything, mate. Lions, Crunchies, Toffee Crisps. That's where I got these Maltesers from.'

Theresa leant forward and hushed us. I ignored her, handing them both a Malteser.

'Say what you like about Secret Tory, and I regularly do, but I have complete faith in his ability to steal from a vending machine,' said Boris. Mrs May leant forward again and whispered pointedly, 'The Archbishop of Canterbury is speaking,'

'... And the second is this: "Love your neighbour as yourself". No other commandment is greater,' said Justin Welby, hypocritically bringing politics back into religion.

'Justin Wokeby,' I whispered to Boris and Keir. I could tell they both got it because their shoulders started heaving as they tried to suppress laughter.

'Will you be quiet!' snapped Mrs May. Everyone looked over. Boris nodded at his security detachment and within moments a mortified Mrs May was being manhandled from her seat and marched down the nave. I leaned over to her husband Philip.

'Hostile environment, hey?'

'Indeed,' chortled Philip.

'Malteser?'

'Don't mind if I do.'

The service was interminable. I entertained myself by seeing if I could nibble the chocolate off my Maltesers without damaging the malty balls inside, and then moved on to a pack of Polos, seeing how small I could get them on my tongue just by sucking, which wasn't very, as I'm an impatient man and I kept mechanically crunching them after forgetting what I was trying to do.

I enjoyed the TV cameras, though, knowing that my flag-bothering colleagues would be beside themselves with jealousy. I just hope they weren't trained on me when my phone went off with the *Match of the Day* theme during the Queen's blessing.

Mingling afterwards, I ended up talking to Tony and Cherie Blair and Everton.

'Fuck me, that went on for ever.'

'Yah, being Prime Minister felt like it went on for ever too, and she's seen fourteen of us,' said Tony reverentially. Cherie squeezed his hand, which annoyed me.

'Oh, well,' I said, detesting every second I was with the talispeople of Cool Britannia

'Go on, then, you're clearly dying to tell us,' I said to Everton.

'I beg your pardon, Mr Tory?'

'These war medals. What are they for?'

'Oh. Nothing, really. I'd rather not say.'

'No, no. You're clearly desperate.'

'I'm not sure I am, Mr Tory.'

'If he doesn't want to tell us I think that's fair,' said Cherie.

'Fair? What do you know about fares unless you're dodging them? No, I want to know where Everton got these medals from that he's so keen to ram in our faces.'

'Secret, please, don't raise your voice,' began Cherie.

'It's OK, Mrs Blair. I can say,' said Everton. 'I got this one for singlehandedly taking out two machine-gun positions on Mount Longdon during the fight to retake Port Stanley, which they said saved the lives of scores of British soldiers, but I was just doing what anyone would have done.'

I shrugged, unimpressed.

'And I got this one for crossing a minefield and taking out a Scud launch site outside Baghdad armed only with a canteen full of rocks.'

'Wow!' said the Blairs, mouths wide open.

'Yes, yes, very good, it sounds very similar to something I did paintballing in Epping Forest last year. We were doing a capture the flag and I—'

'Everton, I don't say this lightly, yah, but I've met a lot of people and it really is an honour to meet you,' Tony said, shaking his hand.

'Thank you, Mr Blair, please don't mention it. I'm just sorry I was too old to help you when you were looking for those weapons of big destruction that naughty Mr Saddam hid so well.'

'WMD,' I contributed.

'Yes, the WMD bombs,' said Everton. 'Where on earth did that scallywag put them?'

'Yeah, where did he put them? Did you ever get to the bottom of that, Tony?' I said pointedly.

He looked satisfyingly incensed.

Cherie interrupted: 'Come along, Care Blair. Justine from Elastica is over there. Let's go and talk to her about Britpop.'

'God save the Queen,' I called after them. 'Here's to another seventy.'

Saturday, 4 June 2022

Another day of festivity for Her Majesty, this time a Jubilee street party in our cul-de-sac.

Despite their Marxist tendencies, the Burkes were using Elizabeth's seven decades of service as a vehicle for their own community-spirited virtue signalling.

It started predictably enough, with people whose only commonality was a postcode mingling nervously until they'd drunk enough Pimm's to relax into talking about themselves.

I held court with some of my recollections of Prince Philip's best gaffes: 'Who do you sponge off? Was this fuse box put in by an Indian? If you stay here much longer, you'll be slitty-eyed.' All his best ones, as well as a few ad libs on the sort of stuff I thought he might have said about single mums, Somalis and gays. Nothing too heavy and very well-received, if the spellbound silence when I finished was anything to go by.

The food was the usual Burke vegan nonsense – mung bean stew, alfalfa salad, chickpea tagine – all that stuff which tastes pleasant but I can't possibly enjoy because it's not the red meat I venerate as if it's intrinsic to my character.

And things took a turn for the worse when, instead of a big patriotic Victoria sponge, the Burkes brought out a vegan cheesecake with a picture of Greta Thunberg on it. Whether it was because of this or the seventh glass of Pimm's, I stood up and roared, 'Her name is Elizabeth

Alexandra Mary the second, there by the Grace of God, of the United Kingdom of Great Britain and Northern Ireland, Head of the Commonwealth, Defender of the Faith, loyal servant to the true emperor, Boris Johnson. Mother to Jimmy Savile's best friends, wife to a deceased racist. And she will have a proper cake, in this life or the next.' We'll never know. But then I staggered up the wrong drive and had a nap behind the Ford Galaxie on bricks at Bill and Jimmy's at number twenty-three. I was woken an hour later by Portillo suggesting that although it was only 2 p.m., I ought to go to bed.

Sunday, 5 June 2022

Ringing hangover, which wasn't helped by the Burkes' maddening windchimes, so I crept into their garden with the kitchen scissors and snipped the bastards. Honestly, in a year of politics, it's the best thing I've done.

Monday, 6 June 2022

Woke to a message from Portillo saying that despite my missing the previous five meetings, there had been some movement on my hostage in Iran. I was on my way to an emergency meeting with her husband at the Foreign Office when the CEO of Sky Bet texted, offering me some hospitality tickets for the New Zealand Lord's Test, so I went to that instead.

I caught up with their chief executive and Ian Botham in the pavilion at lunch, and we had some superb banter, including Beefy texting a picture of his penis to Jonathan Agnew while he was on air.

Tuesday, 7 June 2022

Boring day scrutinising legislation limiting the presence of gambling companies in sport today. Tracey Crouch was suggesting that having bookies' names prominently emblazoned on every sportsperson and stadium in the country normalises gambling for children.

I tried to pay attention, but I kept daydreaming about the delicious beluga caviar and champagne I had in hospitality at Lord's yesterday.

Wednesday, 8 June 2022

Great morning at Johnny's bootcamp. There was something very cathartic about doing star jumps behind Kay Burley while she was interviewing David Davis about today's confidence vote in Boris.

He survived, obviously. Although once my colleagues realise that the number of Cabinet positions he offered outstrips the number available by about thirty to one, for how long?

Thursday, 9 June 2022

I got called into the Home Office for a routine medical today.

Priti walked out with Dr David Bull and ordered me to strip beneath a twenty-foot oil painting of the Duke of Wellington.

Not entirely sure how to address my new girlfriend, I said, 'Hi, baby,' which felt a bit flat when it was still echoing around the cavernous room five seconds after she'd failed to reply.

Then Dr David got to work with a set of callipers.

'Yes, Priti, I'm afraid he is still physically repellent,' he concluded.

'We can all see that. Right, Secret, you need to buck your ideas up: redouble your efforts at the bootcamps or you'll be doing them in Rwanda.'

As I dressed, trying to keep my manhood hidden from the Duke of Wellington's haughty gaze, I concluded that I must have bought a batch of Michelle Mone's diet pills that differed from the ones that gave Steve Barclay a six-pack.

Friday, 10 June 2022

Portillo insisted I do my constituency surgery. I know they say nurses have it tough, but it really is very difficult sitting in my office pretending to be interested in the sort of people I usually cross the road to avoid.

I told myself that three hours of listening to the Toilet Seats' complaints about extortionate bills, unaffordable food and unscrupulous landlords was a small price to pay for the £84k, the second home on expenses, arms dealing, Russian sponsors, Thames Water consultancy, subsidised canteen food and the prestige of being an elected representative.

Everton did most of the work anyway, taking details, committing to get in touch with the appropriate people and keeping me supplied with Tango.

He mentioned that the sagging roof his landlord had held up with a broom handle has now fallen in and that everything he owns is covered in soggy plaster. His poor landlord.

I asked who it was and let out a laugh when he told me: Thérèse Coffey. Who'd have thought her name would crop up in the unfit-for-human-habitation buy-to-let landlord sector? This is the last thing she needs with a baby on the way.

I looked him in the eyes. 'Everton, I'll get this sorted ASAP.'

Didn't get finished until lunch, by which time I was knackered, so decided to take the rest of the day off and ring Thérèse tomorrow.

Saturday, 11 June 2022

Couldn't be bothered to ring Thérèse.

Sunday, 12 June 2022

Ran into Thérèse at a Toby Carvery all-you-can-eat brunch. She was standing in the doorway blowing Café Crème cigar smoke into the faces of families coming in for their breakfast.

'Thérèse?'

'Oh, hi Secret. I'm just doing the black pudding challenge with Mike Graham.'

'How's the …?' I said, nodding at her tummy.

'What?'

'The erm …'

'What?'

'The little one.'

'Oh, the sprog. No, Secret, we went for the twelve-week scan and it was a false alarm. Turns out Gav gave me the wrong thing and I pissed on a lateral flow test.'

'Had he now,' I said thoughtfully.

'Yeah, the daft twat. Neither of us realised what it was because we'd never bothered doing a Covid test before.'

'Well, that must be a relief, anyway.'

'Yes. And it certainly explains why the little plastic box was so difficult to piss on.'

'I'll tell you what, Thérèse, I was worried for a minute when I saw you drinking that pint of Bloody Mary.'

'What? Oh, it's all bollocks, that stuff. I hadn't stopped drinking anyway,' she said, stubbing out her cigar on a laminated menu and dropping it on the carpet.

'Hmm,' I said uncertainly.

'But thanks for everything, keeping quiet with it all. Gavin and I appreciate it.'

'No problem.'

'If there's ever anything I can do for you, just let me know.'

'Well, there is something I've been meaning to ask you, but I've completely forgotten what it is. I'm sure it'll come back to me.'

'Gav and I are sneaking off to his new crenellated caravan in Cayton Bay for the summer, so try and remember before then.' She wiped a trickle of black-pudding blood from her face. 'You know what they say, "When the van's a rocking, don't come a knocking".'

I looked over at her table, where Mike Graham was slumped over a plate of partially eaten black puddings.

'How did you get on?'

'Still undefeated.'

Monday, 13 June 2022

I went back to Golddiggas with a renewed vigour today.

Johnny put us in pairs and we did boxing. I got Jonathan Gullis, which was scary because he hadn't listened to the instructions and was just swinging wildly and screaming, 'Look at me now, look at me now, look at me now!'

Luckily, Johnny saw what was happening and partnered him up with Ben Bradley, in a full Nottingham Forest kit, while I hit the jackpot and got Penny Mordaunt in her Sweaty Betty Lycra.

Gullis and Bradley went at it like they had some sort of point to prove about how neither of them is an intellectually incurious, insecure pillock. Things soon spilled over when Bradley accused Gullis of singing the national anthem only twice a day. Gullis fired back that Bradley hadn't even come to clean Churchill when he'd been graffitied by BLM.

Johnny broke it up while I stood back and protected the ladies. It ended with the three of them rolling onto the ground, with Johnny saying, 'Guys, guys this is supposed to be about personal growth,' as his face was squashed into the grass beneath Bradley's buttocks.

Tuesday, 14 June 2022

Went to the opening of the new HMRC office. It's owned by a tax haven firm based in the British Virgin Islands through an offshore company owned by Tory donors.

Rishi cut the red tape to the sort of delicate applause that can only ring from tax-exempt hands, because they've got enough disposable income to moisturise regularly.

It looked very prestigious and exactly like the sort of thing I should be doing, so I got on the blower to Portillo to demand he arrange for me to do an opening too. He called back an hour later: I'm doing the new dairy aisle at our local Asda next week.

Wednesday, 15 June 2022

Got a letter from Thames Water saying that due to my continued and valued non-executive director work on their behalf, they would like to name a fatberg after me. I told them it would be an honour.

Thursday, 16 June 2022

Watched *Question Time* for the first time in for ever last night. It was the standard 2-1-1-1 panel of government minister, right-wing ghoul, Labour melt, Lib Dem nobody and last public figure you expect to see, like an *Apprentice* contestant or an extra from *Lewis*.

But after they'd introduced Dominic Raab, Ann Widdecombe, Wes Streeting and Tim Farron, my Primula and piccalilli cracker hit the floor. Because the fifth guest, the interesting public figure, the person who was going to speak to us unconstrained by a party whip, was Jodie. Lance Forman had got lost in his own factory and had to cancel last minute, so the producers invited her on after the stir she's been making these last few weeks.

I was livid. I've only ever been on rubbish *Any Questions?* and they haven't invited me back after I tried to put off Diane Abbott by waving a can of piña colada at her. Yet here was someone who works in retail getting to mix with politicians like they were her equals.

When she got to do the 'I don't believe this, Fiona, but I'm actually in agreement with (*insert name*) on this' segment, I had to turn off. The thought of her giving a witty answer to the novelty question was more than I could countenance.

Friday, 17 June 2022

Clips of Jodie on *Question Time* have gone viral. There's one of her doing a monologue, saying that she's worked minimum-wage jobs all her life and Tories who start life with a three-goal head start don't have a clue, and another of her zinging Dominic Raab when he said he'd like to see the return of the death penalty, with, 'What, death by paddleboard?'

She's become a centrist darling, with people like Emma Kennedy giving her the kiss of death by hailing her as a genius. Poor Jodie. She's not savvy enough to realise that until Brexit took all the Remainers' cleaners and au pairs, they didn't know struggling working-class people like her existed.

Saturday, 18 June 2022

Been having a lot of problems with wildlife in the garden recently: woodpeckers, redstarts, swifts, nuthatches, toads, adders, slow worms, badgers, hares, red squirrels – all the pests. I was telling George Eustice about it and the Environment Secretary advised pulling up my lawn and getting some Astroturf down. Apparently, it kills 100 per cent of everything.

Sunday, 19 June 2022

Steve Baker has asked if I've thought any more about joining Conservative Way Forward. He says they're having a summer re-education camp and is very keen that I come. I told him I would, if it weren't for the fact that I'm an old-school pocket-liner who is only in politics for himself.

'We'll see,' he said darkly.

Monday, 20 June 2022

Portillo rang during bootcamp to remind me I was supposed to be taking Elsie in for her elective hip-replacement. He asked if I'd forgotten as Johnny counted me to the end of an isometric squat, and I assured him that I hadn't.

I raced straight back to collect her, pausing only for a post-exercise guided meditation, spinach-and-agave smoothie and goal-setting session.

When I arrived, Elsie was very pleased to see me, Portillo less so. He kept saying that if he hadn't listened to me telling him I was only twenty minutes away for the last three hours he could have put her in a taxi and she'd have been there by now.

Elsie was very grateful, though. I told her not to mention it and to just give me £30 for the petrol.

When we arrived she copped a right earful from an irate Scottish ward clerk who was keen to let her know that the elective surgery list runs on a very tight schedule, so I left them to it and doubled up the errand with constituency work by posing for campaign literature selfies with the patients. A surprising number objected, so I focused instead on the people in traction who couldn't move.

Elsie looked terribly apprehensive when I said goodbye, but there was nothing I could do, so I clapped her on the back and went home.

Tuesday, 21 June 2022

Portillo says they operated on Elsie this morning and it was a success, but that I'd driven off with her overnight bag so could I please go back in and drop it off. I told him this was impossible due to my having just run a bath.

Wednesday, 22 June 2022

Baroness Fox of Buckley has been in touch about the think tank gig. She's invited me to interview for the position of 'thought antenna' at her new policy institute, The Independent Exchange of Ideas Exchange. This is it! I'm going to be the biggest public intellectual since Robert Kilroy-Silk.

Thursday, 23 June 2022

With two by-elections happening in Wakefield and Tiverton today for the relatively innocuous reasons that one of our MPs sexually assaulted a teenage boy and another enjoys watching porn in Parliament, I was frustratingly unable to assist due to opening that new aisle at my local Asda.

It really wasn't the prestigious event I'd hoped it would be, either. There were no local dignitaries or flying champagne corks. Just a gaggle of cost-of-living types (benefit claimants, OAPs, nurses) waiting to get to the reductions shelf, the manager and a couple of bored members of staff. They'd forgotten the scissors for the ribbon too, so I had to use a pair of unsold ones still attached to their cardboard packaging.

But that wasn't even the worst bit. After the ceremony, when I was given a tour by the top-pocket-ink-stains graduate trainee, I skidded in a slick of Elmlea, fell and fractured my tibia.

I was taken to hospital, where they operated immediately. I am writing this from an orthopaedic trauma ward adjacent to Elsie.

Friday, 24 June 2022

The pain of the operation was overwhelming.

I kept having to ring the nurse for morphine. Then I had to ring her for food. Then I had to ring her to demand she sedate the man opposite who spent the whole night saying, 'I'm all right, Jack.' Then I had to ring her to ask who won the by-elections. Then I had to ring her when a male nurse with dreadlocks appeared. Then I had to ring her to ask for a bed pan because the food had gone right through me.

It was 3 a.m. before I could even contemplate nodding off, at which point she had the audacity to wheel her bleeping trolley in and perform post-op observations, so I insisted on making an official complaint. Why the rest of the bay was up in arms when I was the one who couldn't get any sleep, I'll never know.

I loathe the NHS. They may have given emergency care, transported me to a hospital, performed surgery and had me recovering in under twelve hours, but it's the left-wing insidiousness of it all I can't stand. The having to sleep in the same space as poor people, the food from a heated trolley, the nurses singing Nelly Furtado songs on an ancient CD player. I hate it and it has only strengthened my resolve to continue massively underfunding the whole thing until there is no option other than to sell it off.

Saturday, 25 June 2022

Elsie hobbled over from her elective ward to tell me that we'd lost the by-elections and Olly had resigned in a fit of faux-integrity, and to give me the box of chocolates Lucy had saved up to buy her.

I told her that Olly had been educated at a comprehensive and had always been a weak link, and asked her why she was still in the same clothes she'd been wearing when I brought her in, and she said she didn't have any others.

'Oh, yes. I've still got your overnight bag in my car. You'll have to wait until I'm discharged before I can give it to you now.'

'Oh, don't you worry yourself, Mr Tory. It's no hardship.'

'No, I won't.'

I gave her a shoebox full of leaflets. 'Here you go. If you ignore the terminally ill people, I reckon there are 200 prospective voters in these beds. Get to work.'

She reappeared twenty minutes later in a wheelchair pushed by her occupational therapist. I was furious but – incredibly – it was the OT who felt she could give me a dressing-down for sending an octogenarian post-op out on errands.

Sunday, 26 June 2022

The bloke opposite, the one who only says 'I'm all right, Jack', is called Charlie Trilby. He says it in response to anything you say or do near him. It's mildly amusing if it happens to someone else, but if you're watching his gaunt, six-foot-two, seventy-five-year-old frame pissing in your water jug while he's saying it, you soon change your tune.

I rang The Saj to see if he could get him moved, but he told me that having started his career at Deutsche Bank he doesn't really know much about how hospitals work and that my best bet would be to try the staff on the ward first.

Monday, 27 June 2022

Elsie was reading me *The Fear Bubble* by Ant Middleton this morning when the nurses came in to tell her she was to be discharged. What they didn't realise was that she's become so helpful with my feeding, bed baths and urine-bottle emptying that there was more chance of me watching a BBC Four biopic about Sylvia Plath than there was of me letting that happen.

I got her to wheel me up to the nurses' station, where I told them that I was their MP and if they didn't cancel her taxi immediately, they'd all be looking for new jobs by the end of the week.

Tuesday, 28 June 2022

'He's in here, is he?' I heard Ward Sister Manley thunder before she clomped into my bay and ripped the curtains open.

'You're out. Elsie's out.'

'No, no, no, I sorted this yesterday.'

'You sorted nothing yesterday.'

'I did, I spoke to the nurses on the desk.'

'No, you bullied two healthcare assistants into cancelling a taxi. Elsie has passed her physio and OT and is fit enough for discharge. And so, for that matter, are you. I've no idea why you're still here. You don't even need a stick.'

'I do.'

'Do you fuck.'

'But—'

'But nothing. I've seen all the work you make that woman do. She's eighty-eight—'

'Nine.'

'For heaven's sake.'

'Listen, love. I know you're just saying all this to cover yourself, but everyone knows you can go straight back to full activity after a left total hip replacement.'

'She needs to fucking rest. At home. How the hell did a sociopath like you become an MP?'

'You've answered your own question there,' said Mr Trilby.

'What?' I snapped at him.

'I'm all right, Jack,' he replied.

'Pack your things. You're discharged at ten. Or else.'

I nodded in a cowed manner. But I was calling her bluff. She didn't know if I was going to allow myself to be discharged or not. Only I knew that. So even though I was, I had the upper hand.

Wednesday, 29 June 2022

Boring first day back at work. A story broke about Carrie and Boris engaging in oral sex at the Foreign Office and Deputy Chief Whip Chris Pincher resigned for drunken groping.

Had a lot of fun waving my stick at Lisa Nandy during PMQs, though. Until Peter Bone got annoyed when I knocked over his Sanatogen.

Thursday, 30 June 2022

Went over to the Department of Health for a meeting with The Saj about increasing fees for staff parking at my hospital.

Turns out saying things like, 'Oh no, don't hold it open for the disabled person,' whenever a civil servant goes through a door ahead of you has a very enjoyable effect on their sense of public shame.

July 2022

Friday, 1 July 2022

Back into the office. Portillo gave me a massive file of work, which I gave straight to Everton so I could start work on my thank you letter to Wensleydale Ward.

> Dear Nurses and that weird bloke with the dreadlocks,
> Thank you all so much for your diligent care. You should all have wings – because you're angels.
>> Best,
>> Secret Tory.
>
> PS: Enjoy your new parking charges.

Saturday, 2 July 2022

Got a call from Liz Truss out of the blue.

'Hi, Secret. I was supposed to be doing a photoshoot at the new Stratford Westfield but then I thought, *What the hell, you only live once*. So I've ditched my photographer and I'm a free agent. What are you up to?'

'Wow. Hi, Liz. Er, not much.'

'So how would you like to spend the afternoon cruising the M25 in my pink Twingo?'

'Clockwise or anti-clockwise?'

'Anti.'

Bliss.

'Liz, apart from the Renault, it sounds like heaven. But—'

'But what?'

'I can't.'

'You just said you weren't doing anything.'

'I, er …'

'I won't ever ask you to do something like this again, Secret.'

It was the hardest thing I've ever had to do, but Priti's NDA prohibits me from spending unaccompanied time with other women, and there was no way I was crossing her. I couldn't tell Liz that.

'Because I'm watching *Nazi Megastructures*.'

Sunday, 3 July 2022

Priti rang in the middle of the night.

'I'm flying in from Israel. That's a secret. Meet me at Manchester Airport Days Inn at seven.'

I tried to explain that I wouldn't be able to, due to being in bed, but she ignored me.

'Sorry, love. I've had a litre and a half of Monster and it's gone right through me,' I said as she opened the hotel door and I ran straight past her into the bathroom.

'You're late.'

'You know, it really is quite early, Priti. I had to set off at three. Are you not tired?'

'I don't sleep. Why have you got a stick? You know I find disability a massive turn-off.'

'Sorry. Er, babe, would you like to make love?' I said as I emerged and gave the door a considerate waft.

She looked into the bathroom and then back at me. 'No. It's not working. It's over.'

'What?'

'I'm afraid your face is OK but your body remains repellent, and realistically you're not going to be satisfying me sexually for months. I reached out because you seem completely unprincipled and I thought I had feelings for you, but it turns out you'd just triggered some of my excess self-loathing. It's over. Goodbye.'

As she left it felt like a huge weight had been lifted.

Which then flattened me like a cartoon anvil when I remembered that I'd turned Liz Truss down yesterday afternoon.

Monday, 4 July 2022

Got a call from Prince Andrew saying he needed to lie low for a bit and asking if he could stay at mine. He arrived this evening. He's only ninth in line to the throne so I just did a surface tidy.

Tuesday, 5 July 2022

An enjoyable morning experimenting with filling combinations in the Breville, until Andrew trapped the mains flex inside the cheese and pineapple toastie he was making and it blew the machine.

We spent the afternoon sunbathing on the patio and listening to his favourite music.

I was just grabbing a sweat towel for him when Mrs Burke knocked and asked how long 'my guest' was going to be staying.

'How do you know I've got a guest?'

'The security detail on the mini-roundabout and the SUVs clogging up the controlled parking.'

'Oh, right. Why are you asking?'

July 2022

'Well, it's a bit delicate, and I'm not really sure how to say this, but Flora and Miles are still quite young and we're, well, we're not sure we're comfortable with someone like Andrew living next door.'

'What do you mean, someone like Andrew?'

'You know.'

'No, I don't.'

'A paedophile,' she mouthed.

Straight away I knew this was serious. How had I not heard about it?

'Andy, I've got someone here who says you're a paedo. You're not a nonce, are you?'

'Oh, no. No, no, no. I don't even sweat.'

'See,' I said, turning back to Mrs Burke.

'But Secret—'

'I've had just about enough of your meddling, Mrs Burke. Please go home and let Andrew listen to his S Club 7 in peace.'

I went out and threw him the towel.

'So sorry about that, you know what these woke liberals are like.'

'Don't worry, Secret Tory,' he said, mopping his brow while leafing through a copy of *Seventeen*. 'After a lifetime of public service, I'm afraid I'm all too used to people attacking the brand rather than the man.'

— 253 —

Wednesday, 6 July 2022

Ministers are resigning from the cabinet quicker than Boris can replace them, but my interview with Claire Fox's policy institute is tomorrow so I'm ignoring it all. She wants to get away from the image of think tanks as sinister dark-money fronts for malign interests and is looking for a range of earnest seekers after knowledge from across the political spectrum.

During *Hollyoaks* I brainstormed a few ideas with former UK trade envoy Prince Andrew.

He said that criminalising parody Twitter accounts, defunding the NHS and Private Finance Initiative-ing the army into regiments like the Serco Fusiliers and Capita Royal Anglians were OK, but they still needed work. Then he suggested the Quorn laws, a levy on vegetarian food to encourage people to eat more chorine-washed chicken and hormone-fed beef, which is a rubbish idea, so I ignored it and left him to his emotionally incontinent Cheshire teens.

Thursday, 7 July 2022

Baroness Fox didn't want to come across as too pretentious, so the interview was at Shakespeare's Globe Theatre.

I arrived early and looked at the bumph she'd sent me for the first time, a glossy pamphlet with a picture of Toby

Young's head photoshopped onto Vitruvian Man on the cover:

> The Independent Exchange of Ideas Exchange is a cognoscenti hypernode specialising in non-kinetic information transfer. Put simply, we are idea farmers, unafraid to grasp the nettles of controversy while spraying thought-pesticides on the dock leaves of groupthink.
>
> Your interview, held in conjunction with our partners at Aeroflot and GlaxoSmithKline, will be held at Shakespeare's Globe, the birthplace of Romano-Saxon thought. It will involve psychological evaluation, 6G assessment and data transmission. The successful candidate(s) will be rewarded with profile augmentation and £200,050 a year. Together we will expand the frontiers of intellectual enquiry while defending some of society's most marginalised groups: big pharma, petrochemicals and tobacco.
>
> Will you join your fellow Galileos on a voyage to the boundaries of the human mind?

As I put it down, I was astonished to see Jodie walk in.

'What are you doing here?'

'Same as you, I guess.'

'What? You work in WHSmith. You don't get to work for think tanks.'

'Humbled. But I don't any more.'

'Oh yes, that's right. You're a midwife, aren't you?'

'What?'

'Your mate at WHSmith said you're a midwife now.'

'What? Have you been stalking me?'

'No, I was buying more petrol than I needed.'

'Well, I'm not. I'm working for Labour, not people in labour.'

'Wh-what?' (This was involuntary.)

'I'm researching for Lisa Nandy.'

'Bu-but—'

'But what?'

'But … But … You didn't go to any of the right schools or parties. You were never in Living Marxism. Your dad didn't pick up the phone and get you into a university. You don't even know Ghislaine Maxwell.'

'I was on *Question Time* last month and the public seemed to like me.'

'I was on the *Moral Maze*.'

She shrugged.

'But. But what do you even stand for?'

'I'm not sure. What do you stand for?'

'Venality and vested interests.'

'OK, well, I probably stand for the opposite of that.'

I was about to say something incredibly witty which I hadn't yet thought of when I was called into the courtyard of the faithfully reproduced Victorian playhouse.

It was very intimidating. Toby Young, Dominic Cummings, Peter Hitchens and the Fox twins, Claire and

Laurence, sat at a long table, exchanging sideways, highly satisfied glances in a we're-visually-presenting-as-the-six-Trivial-Pursuit-categories kind of way.

They sat in judgement, benevolently firing off their enormous neurons in honour of little old me. I wandered over to an unmanned interval trolley and leant on it. They began writing with quills on their iPads, apart from Toby, whom I noticed was conducting an experiment with some test tubes.

'What are you doing there, Toadmeister?' I asked, wanting to look like I had a keen mind.

'Oh, nothing. Just a bit of quantum physics.' He poured some vinegar on bicarbonate of soda and watched it fizz. 'I like to dabble.'

'Aye, me,' said Laurence, abruptly standing to give John of Gaunt's big speech from *Richard II*, although since he kept forgetting lines and substituting ones from *Lewis*, it lost a lot of its sense.

'Prole! Who is playing Hamlet here in August?' he shouted at an employee who was walking past.

'I'm just a cleaner, mate.'

'And I am Laurence Fox. Tell your boss I'm free.'

Toby patted his back. 'Your time will come, Lozza. Your time will come.'

'Thinkers, thinkers, it is time to consider the mind of a fellow homo sapien,' said Claire, who was wearing a Paedophile Information Exchange tee-shirt.

Peter made a noise from inside his gas mask.

'Commence!' said Toby.

'OK, Secret,' said Claire. 'This is your chance. Level with us. Why do you want to become a thought antenna in the Independent Exchange of Ideas Exchange?'

At this point I remembered that while I am often over-burdened with powerful intellectual thoughts when I'm on my own, or the internet, I often struggle to make any of them come out of my mouth when I'm in public.

Friday, 8 July 2022

Spent the morning in my car port looking at the underside of my bonnet and rerunning the interview in my head.

Just before lunch a scruffy girl in a blue cagoule put her head in.

'Good morning, Mr Tory. I'm a journalist from the *Advertiser*. Would you mind if I asked you a few questions?'

'Yes, I would. Enemy of democracy. Get off my property.'

'I'm not on your property. This is a pavement.'

'I'm the elected MP for that pavement and I'm telling you to get off it.'

'You can't do that.'

'I can.'

'OK. You can, but it has no legal weight.'

I couldn't work out if I'd just won the exchange, so I unscrewed the screenwash cap to make it look like I knew about cars.

'Mr Tory, I was wondering if you could tell me what you know about a company called Joburg Munitions Enterprises?'

'I've no idea what you're talking about. Would you kindly leave me alone? I have very important business with which to attend.'

'Refilling your washer fluid?'

'Among other things.'

'So, you don't know anything about the mysterious disappearance of a case of a chemical weapons antidote called atropine from the Porton Down research facility? The one that mysteriously turned up in the possession of a captured company of Wagner Group mercenaries in Ukraine this week?'

'No. And I've never met anyone called Bruce or Yevgeny either,' I said, before slamming the bonnet on my fingers and unleashing the loudest cry for help in my life.

Saturday, 9 July 2022

Woke in a cold sweat after a nightmare in which I was a corrupt MP doing arms deals with dodgy Russians, about which a local journalist was asking questions. Then I remembered it was true, so I downgraded it to a realistic dream and went back to sleep.

Sunday, 10 July 2022

Toby Young rang while I was outside the local police station waiting for Andrew to sign some sort of register.

'Hi, Secret Tory. Yeah, I'm just reading a bit of Solzhenitsyn.'

'Hi, Toby, I'm thrilled to hear you're reading a bit of Solzhenitsyn.'

'Have you heard of him?'

'Yes. He was an ice hockey player, wasn't he? I'm sure I saw that in a film.'

'Yes, I believe so. Listen, we're not giving you the Independent Exchange of Ideas Exchange thought-antenna gig.'

'Oh, for fuck's sake. You're all the same. Wankers, playing at being clever, poncing around on your little stage, so embarrassingly desperate to make other people think you're smart it hasn't ever occurred to you that genuine intellectual hunger manifests in self-disciplined diligence, not empty posturing, impenetrable language and klaxon-level reference-dropping.' I paused for breath.

'Secret, stop, stop. We're not offering you the thought-antenna gig because we're creating a special position just for you: Emeritus Professor of Brain Insurgency. Your idea about the Quorn laws was something else.'

'Oh, er, yes. Great. Thanks. I didn't mean it, by the way.'

'What?'

'What I just said.'

'Of course not. It was clearly a meta observation on the nature of human endeavour.'

'Indeed,' I said uncertainly. 'Did you give Jodie a job?'

'God, no. You should have heard some of the things she said about equality. Listen, we've got a meeting arranged at the Brentwood Enterprise Centre on Wednesday. Can you make it?'

'Is the Pope Catholic?'

'Always asking questions. I love it. I'll go and do my research. See you Wednesday.'

Monday, 11 July 2022

Boris has resigned and there's going to be a leadership contest after all. I rang Lee Anderson and told him to dust off my campaign literature. Then I called him back and told him to stand down again after a brick came flying through the kitchen window. There was a note attached: 'Bwyta dy Coco Pops a chadwa'n glir o'r ras arweinyddol.'

I opened the front door and said, 'What does this mean, Guto?' as he was getting back into his Honda Civic.

'Eat your Coco Pops and stay away from the leadership race.'

In other news, Prince Andrew has deleted all the saved episodes of *Nazi Megastructures* off my Sky planner so that he could record the last three months of *Home and Away*. We have fallen out.

Tuesday, 12 July 2022

Despite never having gone without the month's rent from him, Thérèse has evicted Everton on the pretext that his constant hectoring about the collapsed roof is affecting her mental health. She's kept his deposit to cover the stress she's suffered because of his tenancy. I can't say I blame her.

He says he has no savings because his forces' pension barely covered the rent in the first place. I told him he should have thought about that before giving Thérèse such a hard time.

Lucy and Elsie offered to let him sleep on the floor of their almshouses, but I said I wasn't having it. This was my responsibility, and I was going to fix it. After a long think, I told him he could stay at Portillo's house.

'What?' complained Portillo on hearing the news. 'Dad, you live in a five-bed detached, four of which are empty and you have a vacant second home in north London.'

'Three. I've got Prince Andrew staying.'

'Dad.'

'I told you not to call me that at work. People will think that employing you is nepotism.'

'On twelve grand a year?'

'Yes. You can't possibly think you're worth that.'

Wednesday, 13 July 2022

My first meeting with the Independent Exchange of Ideas Exchange, a seminar at the Brentwood Enterprise Centre called 'Rehabilitating Reputations: Eugenics and Putin. Victims of the MSM?' I tried not to look too starstruck as I rubbed shoulders with such notables as Daniel Hannan, Dominic Cummings, Julia Hartley-Brewer and Darren Grimes.

We started with a presentation from Arron Banks about Russian money. The car insurance Iago climbed onto a stool: 'Right, the UK and the Ukraine share the first two letters. And this is where the similarities end because Ukraine is to Russia as the Isle of Wight is to England: Russian. It belongs to them.'

Everyone looked a bit baffled, apart from Darren Grimes, who was furiously scribbling notes.

'Who do you think would be living in all those empty Kensington houses if the Russians hadn't bought them? That's right, illegals. Putin has been shielding us from the dreadful liberal urge to offer foreigners sanctuary.'

Darren asked for some more paper, and then Claire opened the floor for questions. This was what I really liked, the smorgasbord of viewpoints, from centre-right to far-right, with a soupçon of so-hard-left-it-was-hard-right for good measure. There's nothing like being surrounded by people who quote Jordan Peterson to make you question *everything*.

Dom Cummings was in his element, loathing every second he had to spend with people he considered inferior while simultaneously thriving on the baffling esteem in which they held him. Julia Hartley-Brewer, reclining on a chaise longue brought in by two rent boys, dazzled us by knowing precisely the most obnoxious controversy-generating position to take in any given situation, while Daniel Hannan spent the meeting pulling a push door, which none of us saw happening because it was for the wrong meeting room.

The session ended with Toby on eugenics. If the essence of oratory can be grasped by the frequency with which six-syllable words are effortlessly shoehorned into it, then this was rhetorical freebase. But Toby didn't overdo it, limiting himself to pausing to look over the top of his glasses for a restrained ten seconds after deploying each one.

As he was approaching the climax of his treatise – '… which is why I am fully opposed to antidisestablishment-arianism …', eight-second pause. 'To conclude, we have spent too much time racing for a cure, when what we need to do is find a cure for—' – the fire alarm and sprinklers went off. Daniel Hannan had finally wrestled open the door, and it was for a fire exit whose sensor required the whole building to be evacuated.

As we elbowed past each other to safety I thought about asking Toby what he was going to say next. But didn't, for fear of looking stupid. I can't imagine it would have been provocatively vile. This was Toby Young, after all.

Thursday, 14 July 2022

After several days of frosty interactions, Prince Andrew and I have agreed he should move out. We both need some space. And I think I'll need mine until I've found out what happened with Hitler's fortifications on Guernsey.

Friday, 15 July 2022

I was in the House of Commons library looking for references to Joburg Munitions Advisory in Hansard, partly out of curiosity and partly out of due diligence to see what the organisation I'd been dealing with for the last six months was like, when a book was withdrawn from the other side of the shelf I was examining, and I found myself face to face with Steve Baker.

'I know what you've been up to.'

Shit, I thought, running through all the things I've been up to this year that could warrant an evangelical library cornering.

'Hi, Steve. I haven't been arms dealing or selling secrets to Russians.'

He pushed an empty plastic lasagne tray through the gap. 'I know about the thefts.'

I examined the tray. 'That's not mine. Look at the burnt bits. I'd have eaten them.'

Steve clicked his fingers. A bedraggled Matt Hancock was pushed from the Nadine Dorries Wing by Des Swayne.

'I'm sorry, Secret.'

'Matt?'

'He's told us everything,' said Steve.

'What have you done to him?'

'Don't worry,' said Des menacingly. 'He's not the first person to have been waterboarded using Mike Fabricant's wig.'

'Now, listen,' said Steve. 'Conservative Way Forward. Our re-education camp during the recess. With everything that's been going on recently, I was wondering if you'd reconsider joining us?'

'I'm supposed to be going migrant spotting in the Channel with Nigel Farage.'

'And I'm off backpacking around Vietnam to find myself,' added Matt.

Steve slapped him. 'Silence, Huel boy.'

Matt whimpered.

'Nigel will be doing that anyway and you don't need to go to Vietnam to find out that you're a tosser,' said Steve. 'I'd hate for news of the pair of you stealing your colleagues' dinners to become public knowledge.'

He had us in the palm of his hand. I just wished I had some dirt with which to leverage him. If only he'd been up to no good by the canal at Christmas, or with Steve Bannon on the Holloway Road. But I had nothing, I knew if I didn't join I could end up as a party pariah, like Michael Heseltine or Rory Stewart. It was one of those occasions when I sincerely wished that a pre-requisite for becoming a Tory MP wasn't spinelessness, because all I could do was mumble a meek, 'Yes, Steve.'

Lindsay Hoyle appeared.

'Steve? What have I told you about loitering in the library? If the researchers have to call me one more time, I swear ...' He tailed off, perennially unable to think of a threat he had the power to carry through.

'Sorry, Mr Hoyle,' said Steve unctuously. He turned back to us. 'See you on the twenty-fourth.'

Saturday, 16 July 2022

Nigel was very understanding about me needing to rearrange our refugee spotting in Margate.

'No problem at all, Secret. Let's do it later in the year. And listen, I'll be out there anyway, so don't worry. It's like I've always said, do a job you love, and you'll never work a day in your life.'

'Thank you for being so kind-hearted, Nige.'

'No worries, buddy. Stay safe. And watch out for economic migrants.'

Sunday, 17 July 2022

I'm in the clear! Geoffrey Cox has defeated the car-parking company who fined me for parking in a disabled bay back in October. It's the best eight grand I've ever spent. Up yours, NCP!

To celebrate, I watched the leadership contest on ITV. It was scintillating stuff, the candidates taking it in turns to see how many times they could say 'deliver' in a sentence – that is, when they had the wherewithal to complete one.

Monday, 18 July 2022

I went back to boot camp this morning. Everyone was talking about CCHQ cancelling the final televised debate because of concerns about the public seeing the very best talent we have to offer being electoral poison.

The session was fun though. I was still quite limited with what I could do, but during the exercises I had to sit out, Johnny asked me to time keep. The others got angry when I instinctively began abusing my power to get them to work longer than needed, but Johnny's constant 'sweat is just your fat crying' patter kept them going. I love the affable way in which he talks to me. After a particularly prolonged plank he quipped, 'Terrible counting, Secret. We'll make a PT of you yet.'

'Or a Treasury minister,' shouted gobby Jess Phillips, nosing around after an interview with Maitlis.

Tuesday, 19 July 2022

Hottest day on record with large swathes of the country on fire, so I sat in my air-conditioned Overfinch on the drive to cool down. Mrs Burke had the audacity to tell me that idling the engine was contributing to climate change, so I revved it until she got upset and went away.

Noticed that the hack from from the *Advertiser* has run the story about me building back better by moving military-grade chemicals into Ukraine via the Wagner Group. It speaks volumes that these so-called 'journalists' are willing to run stories like this, yet nothing about the new dogshit bins in Jubilee Park or the speed camera I'm getting for the bypass.

Wednesday, 20 July 2022

Harry Cole, who is now insisting on training with his top off, got hold of a copy of the *Advertiser* and read it aloud at bootcamp today. The scamp.

'Secret Tory would appear to have been using his parliamentary status and contacts to work as a middleman between a shady South African shell company, the Saudi government and Russian mercenaries in eastern Ukraine. When I interviewed him in his garage—'

'Mock Tudor Car port.'

'—he denied all knowledge of these interactions. But the testimonies of staff at Salisbury Cathedral, Wyndham Sevenoaks Days Inn and the English Heritage Stonehenge visitor centre paint a bigger picture. While Mr Tory's seat commands a 27,000 majority, in recent months he has been next to invisible in the constituency, with sources saying that he regularly meets with Saudi warlords, South African criminals and Ukrainian Nazis—'

'Russian.'

'—while constituency work is done by his son, a homeless veteran and two pensioners.'

'Sounds like a good set-up,' said Dom Raab.

'You don't know the half of it.'

Peston scratched his chin. 'You know, this is really the sort of story I ought to be running on ITN.'

'Same here,' said Nick Robinson. 'But then you think how Secret just saved our shoulders when he counted short in Johnny's military-press challenge and think better of it.'

'Secret, you really are a card,' said Chris Hope. 'Swap me that eight-kilo kettlebell for the twelve and I'll do a cuddly profile on you.'

Thursday, 21 July 2022

I couldn't sleep for worrying about the *Advertiser* story. Thankfully only *Private Eye* has picked it up. This is a relief because it means that the MSM will ignore it for at least two years.

Rishi and Liz are the final contenders in the contest to become the next Prime Minister of Great Britain. Bill Cash was furious, saying that Liz's presence at this late stage represented exactly the sort of charitable inclusivity Tories are supposed to be against.

Friday, 22 July 2022

Last day before recess. Golddiggas was great fun this morning. Everyone has lost varying amounts of weight, and for many of us it has reinforced the significance of hard work. Like being poor, being fat is a choice.

We all have the same twenty-four hours in a day, and if minimum-wage people choose to spend theirs doing overtime on checkouts while eating meal deals rather than visiting £80-per-hour PTs and having high-quality nutrition delivered by Ocado, then that's on them.

In the afternoon the boisterous Redwallers got demob happy and started signing each other's shirts. With their youthful, mildly fascistic outlook, the 2019 intake really has brought a new freshness to parliamentary proceedings.

Grant Shapps joined in. He asked me to sign his shirt with my mother's maiden name, the name of my first pet and name of my favourite sports team. We were shooting the breeze about his new no-risk residual income injection scheme, requiring an initial outlay of only five grand, which I would make back ten times over in the first year because motivation plus skill plus knowledge plus time equals success, when a Mondeo pulled up and the window wound down to reveal Des Swayne in a red beret.

'I hope you've not forgotten about tomorrow, Secret.'

'No, Des,' I gulped.

'Watford Gap, 2 p.m. No excuses.'

Saturday, 23 July 2022

A real scorcher. One of those days when you wish you were going on a holiday rather than to a re-education camp.

We loitered in the car park of the worst services on the M1 northbound, interested to see who else among our colleagues had been singled out for re-education. Sir Gavin Williamson, Thérèse Coffey, David Davis, Matt Hancock, Nadine Dorries, Kwasi Kwarteng and Lee Anderson were all there, as well as Olly Dowden, with his newly discovered conscience, and Ben Elliot, with his long-established enthusiasm for Russian oligarchs.

'What are you two doing here?' I asked

'Steve got hold of a compromising video of me,' said Olly.

'Sex tape?' we all asked simultaneously.

'Audition for *Cats*.'

'Old Deuteronomy?'

'Skimbleshanks.'

'What about you, Ben?'

'Selling state secrets to Russians.'

'Harsh,' said Kwasi. We all nodded.

A British Leyland Sherpa 250 minibus driven by Andrew Bridgen pulled up. Des Swayne in his beret and another man in a balaclava jumped out and began pushing us around and doing that thing soldiers do in films where they tell you to get rid of half your kit because you don't need it.

We filed onto the scorching bus and I sat at the back with Kwasi Kwarteng and Lee Anderson. It wasn't long before they were arguing about whether to have the little overhead fan on.

'Please, Lee, I'm boiling.'

'Kwasi, I'm a naturally cold man. I need it off.'

'Please. I get flashbacks to all my TV studio mortifications when things get too hot.'

'I told you, Kwasi, lad. N-O spells no.'

The man in the balaclava stepped forward. 'What's going on here?'

'Lee won't let me have the fan on.'

'I told him, I'm a naturally cold—'

Before Lee could finish his sentence, Mark Harper – I knew it was him because his name tag was sown into the balaclava – had struck him over the head with a hardback copy of our 2019 manifesto. Lee slumped onto me, semi-conscious. I moved to push him off, but Harper raised his broken-pledge-filled cudgel so menacingly, I froze and opted to allow Lee's drool to seep into the gusset of my chinos instead.

After a long, silent drive we ended up at a farm in East Anglia where we were given a turnip each and billeted inside some dilapidated WWII Nissen huts.

Then we were ordered to assemble in a farmyard that could have been anywhere in England, full of rusty hatch-backs, half-empty tanks of Carbofuran and a large lagoon of putrid vegetable matter that stank of urine.

Steve Baker, every inch the Brexit paramilitary, climbed atop a rusting Vectra the farmer was using as a post box.

'Welcome to the Conservative Way Forward re-education camp. You are here because you have lost your way. Because you have become preoccupied with career progression with a view to ending up on *Strictly* over the annihilation of the state. It is my great hope that here, in the desolate English countryside, you will learn to love your country again. I am a Christian man.'

The heat and the stress were too much, and Sir Gavin fell over.

'Chuck him in the cooler,' snapped Baker. Swayne and Harper dragged Sir Gavin into a three-foot-high corrugated hut.

'No weakness on the parade ground,' clarified Baker. 'Where was I? Christianity. Forgiveness. Brexit! Brexit was supposed to set this country free. But we have singularly failed to impose economic sanctions on ourselves that are harsh enough, and now there are too many jobs that only Romanians are willing to do, and they've all gone home. This needs to change: for the next two weeks I am offering you all a chance to rediscover your Saxon roots and learn what it means to reap Brexit dividends. Turnip-shaped ones.'

Sunday, 24 July – Thursday, 4 August 2022

I tried to keep a daily diary of these days, but the toil was too much. This account is from memory.

'Hands off your cocks, on with your socks, parade ground in fifteen.' Swayne said this at 04.30 each day.

We were in the fields wrenching globular brassicas from Albion's soil from sunrise until sunset. Swayne issued instructions from the bucket of an ancient Massey Ferguson; Harper incentivised us with cracks of a whip

Some fared better than others. Baker had a particular aversion to my one-time campaign manager Lee Anderson, I think because Lee represents the sort of authentic, unguarded working-class champion an ex-RAF man who helped crash Lehman Brothers can never be.

Baker always made him work harder than everyone else. After a week, Lee was broken. Sunburnt, knuckles raw, physically exhausted, mind shattered, the man who had himself campaigned on a platform of sending benefit claimants into the fields now cried at the thought of arable land.

It wasn't just the labour that was hard. It was constantly being on edge.

One evening we were sharing a contraband pork pie that Nadine had smuggled in when Swayne and Harper conducted a snap hut inspection. Despite his protestations, we unanimously agreed to plant the wrapper in Matt Hancock's pocket, and he too was despatched screaming into the cooler.

Nobody wanted to go there.

Not after we saw what had happened to Sir Gavin. He went in a proud fireplace salesman in the prime of life with the twinkle of love in his eyes. He came out forty-eight hours later looking like he'd just gone twelve rounds with the Teachers' Union.

Thérèse Coffey, using all her experience as the ex-finance director for Mars drinks, turned the one dry corner of our hut into a medical bay and became our physician. She tended to Sir Gavin as best she could, gently mopping his brow and softening turnip for his ulcerated mouth by masticating mouthfuls herself then disgorging them to him in the manner of a gull.

They were still trying to keep their relationship a secret, but I think most people had their suspicions, particularly when she gave Sir Gavin a hand job to help him get to sleep every night. I knew it was a hand job because I heard Lee

Anderson say, 'Fucking hell, Thérèse, will you stop giving Sir Gavin a hand job every night? It might help him nod off, but it has the opposite fucking effect on the rest of us.'

While the proximity was difficult in some ways, in others it brought us closer together. We chose a superb leader in the shape of Nadine Dorries. Ex-SAS operative David Davis tried to put himself forward, but his elite military training in exactly the sort of circumstances we were facing was no match for Nadine's experience as the second person to get voted off *I'm a Celebrity … Get Me Out of Here!* in 2012.

Whether it was making sure we were all awake first thing by banging one of her empty Disaronno bottles with a wooden spoon, threatening to nail Matt's scrotum to the floor when he wouldn't stop crying, or keeping Kwasi's spirits up by letting him kiss her handbag picture of Boris in the cockpit of a Eurofighter Typhoon, nobody could have held us together like she did.

The drudgery seemed to last for ever. Until one day, when everything changed.

August 2022

Friday, 5 August 2022

It was 04.25 and I was waiting apprehensively for Swayne to unlock and Nadine to start rattling her Disaronno, when Harper put his head in.

'Ladies. Parade ground at seven. You've got a lie-in.'

Completely institutionalised and unused to the deviation in routine, we assembled apprehensively.

'It cannot have escaped your notice that we have been building you up to break you down,' said Baker. Harper whispered something in his ear.

'Breaking you down to build you up. Well, we've done that. And also, you've harvested all the turnips. The last three years have seen us in unprecedented times. Having banished the tyranny of experts during Brexit, only to start listening to them again during the pandemic, is a cause for national shame. But while the eyewatering public spending during the first year of the pandemic must never be repeated, we can at least take some solace in the knowledge that most of it went straight into our friends' pockets.'

He gave Matt a grudging nod, which seemed to make him stand an inch taller. It was a nice moment.

'But in other realms, net zero, for example, you continue to pander to the weak-minded who lap up scientific consensus about the overwhelming evidence for a three-degree rise in planetary temperatures having a catastrophic impact on humanity's future as if it's real, rather than something that will go away if I take enough money from lobbyists. Now, with his special military operation in Ukraine, our friend Putin has reminded us that we need to end our reliance on renewables. Because net zero comes at an unconscionable cost to the most traditional of Conservative values – the inalienable right to drive a big car.'

'Hence, Magna Carta,' said Des.

Steve looked annoyed but carried on. 'And Brexit. Brexit, Brexit, ah, say Brexit!' You could hear his MEGAchurch training kicking in as he intoned the words at different pitches and volumes. 'It was all going so well. A small group of dysfunctional men getting to play at having a war, liberating us from the shackles of free trade and ending our over-reliance on metropolitan gateway foods like avocado, oat milk and quinoa.'

Des began hyperventilating at the mention of these leftist foods. Steve pointed at him, as if the reaction illustrated his point.

'Shame. Shame on you all! Shame that we have allowed our young to be corrupted by foods that lead to socialism, LGBTQ and the humanities. They should have been eating our glorious turnips.'

For those of us following this deranged rhetoric, the atmosphere was electric.

'The first stage of your redemption was the edification of pulling Britannia's bounty from the earth of this farm I happen to have shares in. The second will come in the guise of a special ceremony. Who would like absolution?'

Our brassica-ravaged hands shot up.

'Shout it. Shout, "I want absolution!"'

'I want absolution.'

'Louder.'

'I want absolution!'

'Louder!'

'I WANT ABSOLUTION!'

Steve raised his hand. The Sherpa minibus stalled a couple of times and was then driven forward by Andrew Bridgen from behind the mountain of rotting vegetables, and we were moved out to an old airstrip at the end of the farm where scores of shipping containers were stacked thirty-feet high.

Our task was to empty them of their unusable PPE and relocate it inside a towering wicker statue that looked a lot like the UK's Chief Medical Officer.

Steve asked if any of us would like the opportunity to take charge of the proceedings for the day. Because Thérèse has been encouraging Sir Gavin to grow as a person, he volunteered himself.

It was gruelling work. Harder even than the turnips. Landlocked Tory stevedores moved millions of pounds' worth of defective PPE up and down ladders, doing their best to get on with it despite the inane ministrations of the former Education Secretary, who did nothing himself.

'How long did it take you to build this?' Kwasi asked Steve as we stacked the last of it inside the gigantic man.

'Most of the pandemic. Some of us were doing important work while the rest of you were building empty hospitals and riding Pelotons.'

'More important than harvesting vegetables?' asked Sir Gavin.

'No. Not more important than that, Sir Gavin.'

Lee Anderson, whose journey on the re-education camp had been most like that of Private Pyle in *Full Metal Jacket*, put down a box of masks and said, 'With the ongoing special military operation by our Russian brothers to secure peace in Ukraine, food security is of the utmost importance.'

'You have come far, young Lee,' said Steve, patting him tenderly.

'The course has opened my eyes, father,' replied Lee.

'Gavin, the country can't afford another year of unharvested turnips,' Steve continued.

'Sir Gavin,' said Thérèse.

'Sir Gavin. This little rite will change that.'

'What rite?' asked Sir Gavin.

'The Brexit blossom came, but the sovereignty fruit withered and died on the bough. The labour shortages must not happen again. And it is my most earnest belief that the best way of preventing this is to make an offering to our god of the sun.'

'Rupert Murdoch?'

'No.' He nodded at the midday sun.

'The *Star*?' asked Gavin.

'No, the actual sun,' said Steve.

'Oh, right.'

'Offering of what?' I asked.

'The most suitable sacrifice that lies in our power. Animals are fine, but their acceptability is limited. A child is better. But not nearly as effective as the right kind of adult.'

'What do you mean, "right kind of adult"?' asked Sir Gavin.

'You, Sir Gavin, are the right kind of adult. You, uniquely. A man who would come here of his own free will. A man who would come here as a virgin. A man who has come here as a fool.'

'A fool?' asked Sir Gavin.

'You are the fool, Sir Gavin – Punch, the great fool-victim of history – for you have accepted the role of king for a day and who but a fool would do that? You will be revered and anointed as a king, you will undergo death and rebirth. The rebirth, sadly, will not be yours, but that of our brassicas.'

'But I'm a Christian,' said Sir Gavin, unconvincingly.

'So am I,' said Steve, equally unconvincingly. 'And that is good. For believing what you do, we confer upon you a rare gift – a martyr's death. You will live again. And so will my turnips. It is time to keep your appointment with … The Whitty Man.'

'No! No, no, no!' screamed Sir Gavin as Swayne, Bridgen and Harper began dragging him towards the monstrous wicker effigy.

'What's going on?' yelled Thérèse, emerging from a DFDS crate with an armful of partially perished plastic aprons full of holes.

'We're appeasing the Sun God with the blood of a virgin,' said Kwasi.

'A virgin? Gavin's not a virgin.'

'What?' exclaimed Steve.

'Gavin's not a virgin,' repeated Thérèse.

'Yeah, he's definitely not a virgin,' said Lee Anderson grimly.

'Des! You and your inclusivity. I knew we should have had single-sex dorms,' said Steve.

They let him go and Thérèse gathered the sobbing Sir Gavin to her bosom. 'What about some of the unbutchered pigs over there?' she suggested. 'Nobody needs them.'

'Fine. Let's burn some fucking pigs,' said Steve.

And so, in our final evening at Steve Baker's Conservative Way Forward re-education camp in Shottisham, we stood around an enormous wicker statue of Chris Whitty and listened to fifty sows scream their last atop a pyre of defi-cient PPE.

Steve stood beside the swirling blue flames, taking deep draughts of the poisonous air.

'Breathe, breathe the acrid stench of net zero. I pray thee Lord, if I have found grace in thy sight, show me now thy way, that I may know thee: and consider that this nation of Tories is thy people, yea my Lord, if I see thy Brexit going astray, I will bring it back unto you again.'

He was seemingly at one with the toxic fire, and we listened to him having his visions for a bit, although it wasn't long before the fumes were so unpleasant that the particulates were in our airways and none of us could hear a word he was saying over the cacophony of coughing. I didn't say so for obvious reasons, but I was secretly wishing I'd kept back a couple of the face masks.

As the blazing Chris Whitty Man collapsed behind him, the Beaconsfield Moses emerged from the flames, arms aloft, waving his stigmatas in the air for all to see. I think he wanted to look impressive, but with his bifocals partially melted across his face, the ash stuck to his sweating forehead and the badly drawn felt-tip pictures of Nigel Lawson on his palms, I'm not sure he quite achieved the look he was going for.

Thus, we returned to our hut, and spent the last night of Steve Baker's Conservative Way Forward re-education camp watching the reflected red glow of profligate Tory waste dancing in the windows.

Saturday, 6 August 2022

We were dismissed at lunchtime on the understanding that we supported anything the burgeoning far-right lunatic fringe of the party asked us to do in Parliament next term. During the debrief I told Steve that I felt like I'd learned a huge amount, although on reflection I also felt like I might have just said that because I wanted to leave.

Sunday, 7 August 2022

Wanted to spend the day decompressing but couldn't because the Burkes have discovered a ley line on their patio and their annoying tie-dye friends all came over to experience it.

Monday, 8 August 2022

Viscount Rapacity, the owner of the grouse moor where I took Jodie, has died. It is a sad day for unelected Lords who only ever turn up to vote out of self-interest. I played 'The Last Post' on my kazoo, then held a minute's silence for him on my doorstep.

Tuesday, 9 August 2022

Went for a ride on the Circle Line followed by a mixed grill with Chris Chope. He told me that Viscount Rapacity's body was discovered by three young prostitutes with whom he was staging an intervention. This was typical of his benevolent nature.

Wednesday, 10 August 2022

The flowers I sent to the Viscount's wife have been returned with a message: 'I hope he rots.' She is grieving.

Thursday, 11 August 2022

It's the first day of the grouse season tomorrow and I'm redeeming a longstanding invitation from Rishi, issued when I killed his dog, to a shoot at the Bolton Castle Estate.

Friday, 12 August 2022

Got a call from Ben Elliot midway through the morning's shooting.

'Have you seen who Labour have announced as their new communications adviser?'

'No'

'Your ex.'

'What?'

'Jodie Henderson.'

'WHAT?' I exclaimed as my shotgun went off and a gamekeeper fell screaming. I walked a little further away so I could hear what Ben was saying.

'Jodie?'

'Yes. Secret, what does she know?'

'Nothing.'

'What if she starts talking up about the wretched stuff you lot get up to on the grouse moor?'

I covered the receiver and pointed at the keeper writhing in agony on the floor.

'Can someone shut him up, please? This is important. What wretched stuff, Ben?'

'All of it. You're going to have to do something.'

'Like what?'

'Cancel her.'

I hung up. Rishi walked over.

'Secret Tory, it's OK.'

'Are you going to say nobody ever died of a broken heart?'

'What? It hasn't gone anywhere near his heart. No, it hit the fleshy part of his thigh.'

'Oh, right, yeah,' I said, remembering the man into whom I'd just discharged my shotgun. 'No, it's Jodie. She's been made head of Labour comms.'

Rishi put his lovely billionaire hands on my shoulders.

'You're a Tory, Secret. There is no time for emotion when power is at stake.'

I looked from the keepers fashioning an improvised tweed torniquet, across the bereft landscape to Julian Lewis and Gary Barlow doing keepie-uppies with a winged peregrine.

'You're right, Rishi.'

I walked over to the bleeding keeper and slid a twenty into his top pocket.

'Thank you, master,' wheezed the ashen man as his friends vainly tried to stem the flow of blood pouring through their fingers. Emboldened by his deference, I pulled out my phone and texted Jodie:

'Watch out. I'm going to anialate you.'

She replied immediately:

'Annihilate.'

Saturday, 13 August 2022

With the gamekeeper in a critical condition in intensive care, I felt comfortable to set off back down south. Richmond to Margate is a long drive, but every mile was worth it because this was the start of my rearranged refugee-spotting getaway with Nigel Farage.

He'd booked me into his local, the Collaborator and Firkin, and we had a lovely evening eating ham, egg and chips, shooting the breeze over the recent spell of good weather, Marine Le Pen and the OTT reaction to Putin's genocide in Ukraine.

Sunday, 14 August 2022

The day started with a safety briefing about the dangers of not respecting the water, and three pints. Then we boarded HMS *Mosley* and set sail beneath a turquoise sky onto the evocatively named English Channel.

Nigel is a wonderful sailor. I enjoyed trailing my hand in the glassy water as herring gulls investigated the wipes, turds and sanitary towels of voters in safe Tory seats. I'm a glass-half-full kind of a guy, and as far as I'm concerned, these are trophies of Brexit: a visual reminder that we are no longer under the yoke of EU tyranny. The thought that one of these floaters could belong to Ann Widdecombe was enough to make the hairs on the back of my neck stand up.

But it was a poor morning for migrant sightings, with only miserable gannets, basking sharks, dolphins and an orca to keep us entertained. Still, as we nibbled a lunchtime round of ham and piccalilli under a cloudless sky, Steve's re-education camp seemed a lifetime away.

After lunch Nigel got out his compass and orientated us towards Windsor Castle for a midday rendition of God Save the Queen – and there off Sheerness, as we sang the last refrains of the national dirge, was a dinghy full of Kurds.

We were soon alongside and my guide Nigel, a sort of Chris Packham of xenophobia, effortlessly reeled off facts about the disorder, Islamification, thieving, drug-dealing and anarchy they wanted to bring with them.

Watching him leverage the plight of some of the earth's most vulnerable people up close was breathtaking, a master-class in animosity disguised as concern. That evening I returned to my lodgings exhilarated and satisfied.

Monday, 15 August 2022

A late start but we were on the water by eight, and Nigel was doing a live Instagram Q&A in front of a tub full of Somalians by ten. He says if he doesn't make it as a Nazi politician, he's considering becoming an influencer.

Tuesday, 16 August 2022

Bit of a downer today. By the time we arrived at HMS *Mosley*, smog from the perpetual nineteen-mile non-Brexit-related HGV tailback on the M20 that they don't have a mirror of in France had reduced visibility to the point that the harbour master was refusing departures.

Wednesday, 17 August 2022

Nigel's protégé Natalie Elphicke came out with us. She's still in the posing-with-empty-dinghies-on-dry-land phase of her training, but Nigel thinks he's spotted raw potential.

The first part of the voyage was lovely. Natalie spoke candidly and with humility about inheriting Charlie Elphicke's parliamentary safe seat after he went to prison for sexual assault. It can't have been easy for her, especially after she was found guilty by a parliamentary standards committee of an egregious attempt to influence his legal proceedings.

But despite her affability and generosity of spirit, she doesn't yet have the nose for a ship full of desperate people that Nigel does, and the closest we came was a lobsterman from Hastings.

Thursday, 18 August 2022

Nigel was back in charge and, true to form, we'd located a RIB of Syrians before the end of John Redwood's first deranged tweet of the day.

'You can take the racist away from the refugees, but you can't keep the refugees away from the racist,' Nigel quipped.

'You're amazing, Nigel,' I said admiringly, at which precise moment HMS *Mosley* started taking on water.

Whether or not it was because I reversed the Overfinch into the fibreglass hull when I drove onto the beach to drop off my sandwiches because I couldn't be bothered to walk this morning, we will never know. But one thing was for sure, we were in trouble, not least because Nigel refused to issue a Mayday.

'I'd rather sink than ask for help from those Marxist RNLI wankers,' he growled.

There was further cause for alarm when we discovered there was only one lifejacket, but with typical pluck Nigel said he'd take his chances with my haemorrhoid ring.

The next five minutes were a blur of panic, icy cold brine and Nigel screaming about French mackerel, but it was the ignominy of being rescued by the very refugees we were trying to repel that will haunt me.

As they pulled us aboard I tried to stamp our authority by talking loudly about British things they wouldn't understand, like Heston Blumenthal and the M4 Corridor, but I was shivering so violently I could barely speak.

They put their blankets and jackets on us to warm us up, and beneath a man called Raheem's LA Gear tracksuit top, I discovered that, on a one-to-one basis, Syrians weren't too bad after all.

He rubbed me enthusiastically, gave me his last Rolo and told me that he used to run an ice cream shop in Aleppo. It was his dream to open another on the M4 Corridor; he loved Heston Blumenthal, and if he ever managed it, he'd love to show me how to make his special-recipe salted caramel. At least that's what I think he was saying. We'd just reached the shore and UK Border Force agents had him on the floor in a headlock.

I know I've been repeatedly pressing for them to behave like this, but the officers were particularly uncompromising, and I was taken aback by the amount of ID they wanted to see from me to prove who I was. It was only when Nigel started a TikTok livestream and all the agents got notifications that it was happening that they believed who we were and let us go.

Friday, 19 August 2022

The last day of my magical week, but with no boat, Nigel took me for a debrief in a greasy spoon instead.

'You've got a great product here, Nigel. You've spotted a gap in the market and I honestly don't think anyone else is doing this.'

'Yes, I'm hoping it'll take off like coasteering. If we can tap into the stag- and hen-do market, I really think the sky's the limit.'

'What are you going to do about a boat, though?'

'Well, that's it, isn't it? I'm going to have to get a new one.'

'How long will that take?'

'I don't know. Nobody's bankrolling me at the moment. Three months of Cameos? Two on the seedier platforms. That's how I afforded *Mosley*. But I'm a bit hesitant. I was absolutely red raw after a month on OnlyFans.'

He gave me a short appraisal form to fill in. Under the positives I put attention to detail, opportunity to defend our women from infidels and knowledgeable guide, and under negatives I put too much wildlife, one-hour detention by UK Border Force, likeable migrants.

That last one really did leave a bitter taste. It's difficult to maintain a high level of hostility towards foreigners when they strongarm you into seeing that they're human beings with the same hopes and dreams as the rest of us.

Saturday, 20 August 2022

Household admin. *One of the great things about being an MP*, I thought as I deleted the ninety-two messages from Portillo about constituency business on my voicemail, *is switching off from your responsibilities for the summer.*

He cycled over in the afternoon with some bad news anyway. Everton has quit. I demanded he tell him he has to work thirty-two weeks' notice, but Portillo said that this would be unlikely as we've never paid him.

Sunday, 21 August 2022

Jodie was in the *Observer Magazine* talking about her meteoric rise from WHSmith sales assistant to head of Labour comms in less than eleven months. It was a puff piece with all the usual nonsense about working-class people who've been on journeys. Why do they never focus on the real heroes, Tories who start at the top and then just move around a bit? Moving from journalism to politics or banking to a policy unit: that's the real triumph over adversity.

Monday, 22 August 2022

MOT and service day. The best day of the year. I'm a platinum partner at Sculthorpe's, my local Range Rover dealership, which means I get a choice of newspapers and unlimited machine coffee in a special members' area while I wait.

Annoyingly, however, the machine was broken today and nobody had bothered to get any papers in, so I was browsing a week-old *Sun* with a lumpy Kenco delivered by a bleak sales rep in a sticky mug, and it really didn't feel like the executive experience for which I pay two hundred quid a month.

I wandered outside and crossed the road to the news-agent. And stopped dead. My face, which has definitely lost a bit of weight since Johnny's bootcamps, was on the front of every national paper.

Left-wing hacks at the *Guardian*, *Times*, *Telegraph*, *Sun*, *Mail* and *Express* had belatedly picked up on last month's story in the *Advertiser* about how I levelled up my constituency by helping get that atropine into Russian hands on the Ukrainian battlefield.

By the time I returned to the dealership, it was surrounded by journalists.

Discretion being the better part of valour, and dodging scrutiny the most important part of being a legislator, I hotfooted it home, where there was also a media presence outside my house. I sneaked into the Burkes' garden, taking great pleasure in trampling on their Malala mural before I tentatively poked my head through the branches.

A pap shouted, 'There he is, get him!' and camera shutters began firing at me like an Atlantic Wall MG42 nest on D-Day.

Remembering that the window of the Aitken Suite was still open from this morning's pancracker, I made a break for it, commando rolled across the lawn and posted myself headfirst through the UPVC slot. I've never been so glad to see pube-bearded porcelain and three empty bottles of Toilet Duck in my entire life.

I took stock. The national press was ensconced, and, if I wasn't mistaken, being supplied with sandwiches and cups of tea by the Burkes.

Tuesday, 23 August 2022

Woke at seven, peered outside. They were all still there. But I had a train to catch to the Viscount's funeral and nothing was going to stop me giving the Misogynist of the Moors the send-off he deserved.

I opened the car port to create a diversion and went route one, straight out of the front door. I thought I'd got away with it, too. Then I tangled with the Burkes' new wind-chimes.

'Secret Tory, is corruption endemic in the Tory Party?'

'Secret, you're not in the pocket of the Russian government, are you?'

'Mr Tory, do you have any resident parking vouchers?'

'Secret Tory, did you shoot pheasants with Saudi arms dealers?'

'Secret, did you sell Novichok antidotes to the Wagner Group?'

'Yes, I mean no; yes, I mean no; yes, but park in zone C, it's only controlled between ten and twelve and they never check; no, they were grouse – and no comment,' I shouted over my shoulder as I hightailed it to the high street.

The combination of Johnny's bootcamp and two weeks of

turnip harvesting meant I was the fittest I'd been since my abattoir days, and I'd shaken most of them off by the bypass.

I arrived at the station twenty minutes later, panting, saturated in sweat, but happy to be there. My travelling companion looked me up and down and handed me a can of the Lewis Hamilton Monster.

'It used to happen to me all the time. It's amazing how quickly you get used to finding *Mirror* hacks shitting in your rhododendrons,' said Jeffrey Archer.

He was incredible company, just the person I needed on a day like today, reflexively sniping at anyone who dared to peer over their paper at us.

'What's your problem, love? Never seen a pair of corrupt Tories before?'

The funeral itself was a low-key affair – full military honours in York Minster, even though the Viscount had never been in the military – and we listened to Prince Andrew's eulogy about his lifelong passion for eviscerating wildlife and sex workers, and Jeffrey reading his favourite lesson from the Book of Revelation:

'And the fifth angel poured out his vial upon the seat of the beast; and his kingdom became dark, and they gnawed their tongues for pain: and they blasphemed the God of heaven, because of their pain and wounds.'

He pointed at the Great East Window where the scene is depicted, and we looked at the stained-glass sinners munching their own tongues, the day of judgement and the end of time itself.

The coffin was then carried out by a selection of the Viscount's young female friends dressed as maids, nurses and policewomen. I recognised two of them as Dagmar and Svetlana from the shooting weekend in October. Afterwards, they invited us for a respectful drink in the Viscount's favourite strip bar, where we discussed the moving service and apocalyptic stained-glass over a lap dance.

'No, the end of time, this linear Christian time, it does not exist,' said Svetlana, who was funding her PhD in Quantum Gravity at Manchester by cavorting in front of wretched men. 'The distinction between past and future isn't real, it is a consequence of our underdeveloped brain software. Only in our meagre human minds.'

'Oh, how perfectly cute,' said Andrew, patting her on the head.

Jeff leant back in his chair, arms behind his head. 'Have you girls heard of a little old thing called time's arrow?'

'They probably think that's a pop band,' I said, even though I hadn't heard of it either.

'Did you know,' said Prince Andrew in that uniquely annoying way people who announce this fact always say it, 'that you can shoot a Scotsman with an arrow from these walls after 7 p.m.?'

'Somebody ring the SNP!' quipped the eponymous Archer.

'Time's arrow refers to the second law of thermodynamics. The entropy of a closed state always increases,' said Svetlana.

'Like how we run Britain?' I asked.

'Exactly. It is the direction in which time appears to travel,' she said. 'But this is the Newtonian way of seeing. In the quantum realm, time and space are the same thing. It is everywhere and nowhere at once.'

There was a pause as we all sat in silence, not understanding a word she'd just said.

'Do you like *Hollyoaks*?' asked Prince Andrew.

Wednesday, 24 August 2022

When I woke up, on a bench in York station, Andrew, Jeffrey, the girls and my House of Commons lanyard were nowhere to be seen. I put it down to being one of those twelve-hour bender blackouts that are a consequence of encouraging young women to ply you with spiked drinks, bought a cheese and tomato baguette from Upper Crust and caught the train home.

As I was looking for my seat the inevitable git who only realises they need to get their Lilt, lip balm and laptop from their bag once it's been wedged behind three holdalls and a suitcase stood up in front of me.

Sighing loudly, I waited and scanned the carriage. And then I saw her: Jodie, all glammed up like she'd just got the Labour comms gig. A flicker of something that I definitely didn't find intrinsically annoying flashed across her face.

She was surrounded by a team of people working on fancy screens on stems. I was secretly impressed. It had never occurred to me to use a train journey for work. One of her team was conducting simultaneous conversations on a pair of Bluetooth earpieces. I looked closer.

'Everton, what the hell are you doing here?'

He touched each earpiece in turn. 'Be right back. Be right back. Hello, Mr Tory. Ms Henderson offered me a very generous remuneration package to work for her, which has come in very useful since I got made homeless by poor Mrs Coffey. I hope you don't mind.'

'Mind? I'm livid. Why don't you want to work for me?'

'Ms Henderson is very kindly paying me, Mr Secret, and I did have to take that into account.'

'Judas.'

'You've let a good one slip through your fingers here, Secret,' said Jodie. 'But I guess you've got bigger things on your mind, what with still being on the front of every news-paper.'

With the effects of my hangover suddenly very pronounced, I pushed past the annoying aisle blocker and stormed down the train to find my seat.

I returned ten minutes later, having belatedly discovered that my seat was in the same carriage as Jodie. I tried to make it look like I was busy, but with no laptop I had to make do with spreading out the contents of my pockets –

wiretap, rainbow eraser, a copy of *Extreme Ownership* (a book of Navy SEAL combat anecdotes that translate into lessons for business) and a pregnancy test – on the under-sized fold-down table.

At Newark North Gate, Jodie stood up to go to the buffet car. I pretended to take a call.

'Are you pretending to take a call?'

'No.'

'Sure?'

'Fine. Yes, I am. Well, I suppose congratulations are in order.'

'If you like.'

'Congratulations, then. You know, Jodie, I'd have given you the world. But your loss.'

'What?'

'We could have sorted things out. Like adults. But instead I can see you've chosen to take petty revenge on me by poaching Everton and becoming head of comms for a party whose identity is built on not being Tories.'

'Revenge? You think I've taken the best opportunity I've ever been offered to get at you?'

'Yes.'

'Get over yourself, Secret. This is my one chance. At anything. Normal people don't get to pick and choose the well-numerated, varied and challenging jobs. This country is full of people in dead-end employment who have no idea how intelligent they are because nobody has ever told them. I've been given a chance, and I'm taking it.'

'Yeah, I get it. Keir is making Labour a safe space for mediocre careerists and you want a piece of the action.'

'Oh, I know that having been unable to afford to do three internships I'm not the usual type, but as a working-class woman who thinks going to bingo is normal rather than some sort of voyeuristic experience, I'm giving them the sort of credibility that the kombucha-supping MPs commuting from Highgate to safe seats in Doncaster can only dream of. I'm not stupid, I know nobody really gets into politics to make a difference, but at least in Labour they're not *trying* to turn everything they touch to shit.'

'But what about us?' I asked.

'Us? We went on three dates during which you ignored, belittled and humiliated me. There never was an us.'

'I gave you some chocolates.'

She reached into her bag. 'Here, have a fucking Twix. Maybe you can swap it for some spice in Belmarsh. Good luck, you're going to need it.'

I arrived home that afternoon. The media circus was still outside my house.

The demands of the last twelve months began to swirl. Everything became confused. I'd bought a rotisserie chicken for one from Tesco Express and began swinging the carrier bag around my head and running at the accountability roaches.

'I'm mad as hell and I'm not going to take it any more!' I shouted. Michael Crick stepped from the huddle and put a microphone in my face. I didn't even hear what he said, I just swung my bachelor's handbag and knocked him to the floor, ran up my drive and slammed the door.

Thursday, 25 August 2022

The media presence seems to have increased.

Friday, 26 August 2022

I have been placed under house arrest by the MSM. I'm a prisoner in my own home. It's like the Millennium all over again.

As of 3 p.m. today I have watched more than thirty episodes of *Come Dine with Me*.

I was just fantasising about being invited onto the celebrity version when The Saj texted to remind me I was supposed to be doing a real Come Dine with Me for my Black and White Ball prize tomorrow night.

I pressed the phone to my ear with my shoulder, peered out at the journos and then into the bare store cupboard.

'All good, The Saj. Tell them to come over for seven.'

Saturday, 27 August 2022

In many ways it was an odd dinner party.

Anastasia Volkov was the successful bidder. As for the other guests, I'd arranged for Gary Barlow and, to add a sprinkling of stardust, Neil Hamilton.

Anastasia was upset about the paps and Gary complained that they gave him flashbacks to the 1993 Everything Changes tour, but Neil, who thrives in hateful circumstances, relished every second.

My menu was as follows:

Starter
Partially eaten rotisserie chicken

Main
Jar of hotdog sausages
Pot Noodle (Bombay Bad Boy)
Canned mushrooms

Pudding
Angel Delight

The first two courses didn't go down well. At least that's the impression I got when Gary and Neil went grey and took it in turns to visit the Aitken Suite, but the upside was that it afforded Anastasia and I the opportunity to discuss Anglo-

Russia relations and that time I gave one of her operatives *Command & Conquer: Red Alert* rather than a dossier of Tory dissidents.

Gary and Neil returned for the butterscotch Angel Delight, and to my delight, it was a triumph. None of my guests had eaten one before, so I passed it off as my own creation and pretended that was why the other courses had suffered.

In keeping with the spirit of the original Endemol *Come Dine with Me* format, they all then had a nose around my house, which was quite jolly until they happened upon the decomposing pigs' heads on my bedroom floor.

But I think I won them back over when I led them outside for my showstopper party piece: fireworks courtesy of a Joburg Munitions and Sons M240B machine gun.

I fired it straight up in the air, producing a lovely tracer effect which had the pleasantly unanticipated result of terrifying the embedded media.

'Patriotism one, scrutiny nil,' I yelled, as illegally procured shell casings rained on their annoying gazebos.

As I attended to the dishes and fantasised about my guests holding up scorecards of six and above in their Ubers home, there was a flash, bang, shout – and darkness.

Monday, 29 August 2022

The bag was taken off. Faces were looking at me. I couldn't make them out due to the floodlight in my face.

'Is this about the parking ticket?'

'Don't get funny.'

'Oh right, it's just that—'

'Why does an arms company with connections to Russian mercenaries keep transferring money to an elected British MP? Why have operatives begun blackmailing us to say that they have access to the UK Parliament and they know how the Trident codes work? And why, for the love of God, are you firing military-grade weaponry in your garden?'

'You're the specialist investigators, you work it out.'

The bag went straight back on.

Tuesday, 30 August 2022

I am brought out at regular intervals and asked the same questions on repeat. Using the skills I've acquired from decades in front-line politics, I fail to answer a single one.

Wednesday, 31 August 2022

In a bid to break me, Guantanamo Bay-style, my abductors have begun broadcasting deafening happy hardcore in my cell. The joke is on them. I love Hixxy and Sharkey.

September 2022

Thursday, 1 September 2022

That said, by Dougal's effort on *Bonkers 6* I was beginning to wobble. But then, just as I was about to break, the bag was removed and I saw the faces of my interrogators for the first time. There was a knock and Boris walked in.

'Ill met by moonlight, proud Tory.'

'All right, boss. I'm not moonlighting.'

'That's not what I said.'

'OK. But if I was, I'd definitely put it down as a second job,' I said, pleased I'd finally come up with a decent gag to put in my diary. 'I've not really been paying much attention over the summer, boss. Are you still PM?'

'Let's not talk about that now, I've got a chemsex party at Evgeny's to get back to. Listen, Secret, the team brought you in because of that piffling .30 cal light cannon you were firing underneath three flight paths, but these MI5 gloom-sters have a few questions they'd like you to answer on a few other subjecteroonys too: arms dealing, Russian mercenaries, PPE contracts, what Steve Baker's up to, that sort of stuff.'

'What's in it for me?'

'Well, if you're guilty of half the things we suspect, you can go home and carry on like normal because anything else would just reflect so extraordinarily badly on the rest of us.'

I cleared my throat, stood up, got told to sit back down again, and said, 'I took risks. I knew I took them; things have come out against me, and therefore I have no cause for complaint, but bow to the will of Providence, determined still to feather my nest to the last.'

And then I sang like a canary.

Friday, 2 September 2022

Home again. The slate is clean. We've pinned the Dissident Dossier leak on Portillo. He'll do five years, tops.

What a year! If I was writing it as fiction to a publishing deadline I don't think it could have been half as far-fetched.

Saturday, 3 September 2022

Parliament reconvenes on Monday. After a summer in which I went on a re-education camp, saw my ex-girlfriend head up Labour's comms team, sank and got arrested by MI5, I can't wait to meet our new leader and get back to the bread-and-butter Westminster business of looking out for number one.

I bloody love being a Tory.